BREAKING THROUGH

A CHRISTIAN'S JOURNEY TO NETWORK MARKETING SUCCESS

ROD NICHOLS
GEORGE MADIOU

FOREWORD BY *NY TIMES* BEST SELLING
AUTHOR, CHRIS WIDENER

Publishing Coordinator – Sharon Kizziah-Holmes

Paperback-Press
an imprint of A & S Publishing
A & S Holmes, Inc.

ISBN -13: 978-1-951772-69-7

Acknowledgements

Rod Nichols – This book is a very special collaboration. It began in 2007, as God connected George Madiou and I in this amazing project. Now, fourteen years later, the book is finally published. I first want to thank my Heavenly Father for loving us so much that He sent His only Son to die for our sins. Next, I'm eternally grateful to my Lord and Savior, Jesus, for salvation and for the Holy Spirit who guides me in everything I do.

Karen, my wife of nearly 33 years is a true gift from the Lord, my beloved, and best friend. She is also our book editor. I want to thank her for her love and support. Working with a temperamental author can be difficult at times, but she handled it beautifully. Her tireless hours of editing have made this a better book.

Finally, I want to thank my friend and co-author, George. He is a highly respected pillar in network marketing and his magazine, the Network Marketing Magazine, is one of the best resources in the industry. I love his heart for the Lord, the way he is guided by God, and his love of network marketing.

George Madiou - There are many people to whom I am grateful. I have been in the network marketing industry for decades. I have met literally tens of thousands of people that have shaped my 50-year entrepreneurial journey, both this pre and current MLM ride. The most important person that I want to acknowledge is the greatest networker that has walked this earth and that is Jesus Christ. Through him my life has been GBG every day (Guided by God) and I have been guided in spectacular ways, daily.

The very next person is the love of my life Debbie Madiou. 42 years ago, Debbie was a gift given to me, directly from God. I could never count the many ways God's gift has made me appreciate the gift he has graced me with. One of the most significant was the incredible care that I received from Debbie after a recent quadruple bypass, during which I lost 4 months of my "normal" life. Debbie was incredible beyond description.

One of the most special people I've ever met in the network marketing industry has been my friend and partner Rod Nichols. Rod's wisdom has guided so many networkers to success. Rod has been a great author in my magazine.

www.TheNetworkMarketingMagazine.com.

We have worked on a number of projects, but one of the most fun collaborations came to life after years, at the "right time", and it's the book that you are holding in your hand. I'm so glad that I can help share Rod with the networking world and borrow a little of Pastor Rod for our industry. Rod has such a great way of sharing the Word.

I want to also acknowledge you. I pray that you get as much value out of this fun story as Rod and I have.

God bless each and every one of you!

Rod and George want to also acknowledge and thank Sharon at Paperback Press for all her good work to prepare this book for publishing and to Jaycee Delorenzo for the excellent cover design.

CONTENTS

Foreword by Chris Widener

You are going to love this book! I have realized the power of stories ever since I was a child, when I first began to read and listen to stories. Isn't it interesting how when we are kids so much communication comes to us through stories and yet as we get older, we begin to read nonfiction more than the stories? It's interesting to me because so many truths can be communicated through the telling of stories. I've written a number of fictional stories that help people understand the basic truths of the topic of this book. My book, the *Angel Inside*, was a New York Times and Wall Street Journal best-selling book about a young man on vacation in Florence, Italy, who meets an old Italian man who teaches him life lessons from the life of Michelangelo. *12 Pillars*, which I co-wrote with the legendary Jim Rohn, tells the story of a man struggling with his career who gets connected with another man who teaches him the secrets of wealth and success. People love stories and I know that you are going to love this book by my friends Rod and George, *Breaking Through: A Christian's Journey to Network Marketing Success*.

In this story, we learn the lesson of the original networker, Jesus, from the perspective of Paul, the primary character. And the lessons are incredible. Lessons that can change your network marketing career trajectory, and your life!

You will learn the truth about what really happened in the Garden of Eden and how it has affected everyone on earth since then. But you will also learn that we do not have to live under the curse! The fact is that work doesn't have to be a toil. It can be filled with the great blessings of God and something that we enjoy entirely. We can live out our career mission with purpose and passion.

You are also going to enjoy the chapters on Jesus as the Prospector, Presenter, Trainer, and Leader. Rod and George, through the power of storytelling, guide you to understand that what Jesus did, you can do as well. You too can be a dynamic prospector, presenter, trainer, and leader.

We all want to be successful in life and business. Network marketers want to be successful in network marketing, right? That just makes sense. The power of this book is in the fact that it teaches us that if we follow the ways of Jesus, we can find success in our network marketing business because the principles of network marketing are as old as the principles of Jesus himself. For example, I was mentored personally for seven years by Jim Rohn. Jim was renowned for using the scriptures to teach people how to do network marketing. In fact, I was one of the speakers at Jim's memorial service, along with other notable speakers like Anthony Robbins, Les Brown, and Darren Hardy. I read the story of the sower and the seed from the Scriptures, which was one of Jim's favorite passages from the Bible. That passage tells us that some of the seed, in fact most of the seed, falls on ground that doesn't allow it to grow, but the seeds sown into the good soil produces 30 times, 60 times, and even 100 times more than the seed itself. Great lessons there.

The Bible is filled with principles that teach us how to do business God's way. Rod and George, in this compelling book, teach us the principles of Jesus as the original networker and how we can apply those same principles to our own lives. I know that they work, because I've used them in my own life and in building my own businesses.

The Bible teaches us that we are to seek first the Kingdom of God and His righteousness and all other things will be added unto us. What an incredible promise! And yet it is a daily discipline to seek first the Kingdom of God. *Breaking Through* is a tremendous reminder on how to build your business God's way! Dig in deep, read it over and over a few times, and especially pray over the principles that you read and ask God to help you implement them into your life so that you can experience the success that you desire - and deserve - in your network marketing business.

My first company, that I sold to my business partner, was called Made for Success. I called it that because I truly believe that the reason we were created by God is to succeed here in life. Now that doesn't mean that everyone ends up driving a Ferrari. Success isn't just financial. It includes financial but it is also all of the areas of life. *Breaking Through* is a great reminder that you were Made for Success!

One

The Eden Factor

Tim sat, elbows on the desk, rubbing his temples and staring at the phone. After a long day at a job he hated and the umpteenth argument with his wife over the viability of network marketing, following up on a prospect was the last thing he felt like doing. *Probably just another rejection, like the last ten.* He picked up his cell phone. His hand trembled and tongue stuck to the roof of his mouth. He dabbed at a dribble of sweat on his forehead and took a deep breath. The phone felt like a hundred-pound brick. *They probably won't answer,* he reasoned and with a big sigh set the phone on his desk. *Maybe she's right . . . maybe I'm just not cut out to be a successful network marketer.* He gritted his teeth. *I sure hope this convention gives me the spark I need, otherwise I'm done.*

Standing in the first-class section waiting to move forward, Tim gazed at the smiling people sitting in big cushy seats with lots of leg room. A flight attendant catered to their every need. *Man, it would be nice to be in first class instead of sardine class,* he mused. *Once I hit it big in network marketing, I'm never sitting in coach again.* Finally, the short balding man and his wife finished stowing their carry-on bags and the line began to move. He hoped that no one was sitting in the middle seat, so he could have a bit more room and wouldn't have to talk with anyone. Seat 32c was near the back and he had lots of time to think before arriving at his row. He sighed at the sight of a stately looking man with a full head of silver hair sitting in the middle seat and an attractive middle-aged businesswoman in the window seat. After finding a spot for his carry-on, he plopped into the seat and secured his seatbelt, trying not to make eye contact with his seat mate.

"Hi, I'm Paul, are you heading to Maui for business or pleasure?" the man asked.

"Uh, I'm Tim and I'm going to a business convention."

"You'll love Maui, it is truly paradise. What kind of business?"

"Oh, uh, I work with a company that distributes nutritional supplements."

"Network marketing, by any chance?"

"Why yes, how did you know."

"An educated guess. I've been in the industry for thirty years."

"Wow, I've never known anyone who has been in network marketing for that long. You must be very successful."

"Yes, I've done quite well, but I'm retired now and enjoying the fruits of my labor."

"Really, so you don't work anymore?"

"I work, just not in network marketing. I'm also a pastor."

"I'm a Christian too. This is amazing. I've never met any successful Christian network marketers and was actually beginning to wonder if I should even be in this type of business."

"What do you mean?"

"Well, I've struggled with all the greed I see in network marketing. You know, all the big houses, sports cars, boats...ugh. Makes me sick! Particularly when I think about all the starving people throughout the world. Do you know what I mean?"

"I know the feeling well. I too struggled during my early years."

"Really, how'd you get beyond those feelings."

"Well, I recognized that God had a plan to prosper me and network marketing was the vehicle He wanted to use."

Tim cocked his head. "What do you mean God wanted to prosper you. How'd you know?"

"In the book of Jeremiah, it says 'For I know the plans I have for you,' declares the LORD, 'plans to prosper you and not to harm you, plans to give you hope and a future.'"

"Really? I guess I've never read that scripture. I didn't realize that God wanted me prosperous. In fact, I've always had the feeling that it was better to be poor and that it was impossible for rich people to get into heaven."

"Where did you get that idea?"

"Didn't Jesus say that it was impossible for a rich man to get into heaven?"

"Yes, he did say something similar to that, but what he meant was that it's impossible for a person to have money as their god, instead of the real God, and still get into heaven."

"But doesn't the Bible say that money is the root of all evil?" he asked.

Paul chuckled. "No, actually it says that the love of money is the root of all evil."

"Wow, I never knew that. This is quite eye-opening. So, God really wants me prosperous?"

"Yes, in fact it's part of his plan for your life. It was what God intended for mankind right from the beginning. I'm sure that you know the creation story from Genesis, right?"

"Yeah, I guess so, but how does that relate to God wanting me prosperous?"

"Do you mind if I tell you a story?"

"No, go ahead," he replied.

Paul had to wait a few minutes while the flight attendants showed the security procedures and secured the plane for takeoff. He then began telling Tim how in the beginning, when the Spirit of God was hovering over the dark void, God spoke light, but that it wasn't the sun or moon light, as we think of it. Rather it was the light of life and prosperity. So, when God created the earth, its foundation was life and prosperity, which means completeness or not lacking anything. Next, God created a self-producing, self-fulfilling system that would provide for the people he would create. When the earth's ecosystem was complete, God created man in His image and likeness and placed him in that system, known as the Garden of Eden, to rule the earth as His coregent or steward.

The self-fulfilling system included trees and plants that produced the oxygen mankind needed to breathe. Some of those trees produced fruit and seeds for more trees. The plants produced vegetables and grains for food, and again seeds that produced more plants. All that mankind would need to survive was easily available.

The first man, Adam, would live forever and had everything he needed, including a beautiful wife, Eve. Adam and Eve lived in paradise, walking and talking with God, and would never have to work a day in their lives. There was only one rule. They were forbidden to eat from the tree of the knowledge of good and evil.

Then, along came the snake and deceived Eve into believing that if she ate from the forbidden tree she would be more like God. Adam went along with the ruse and sin and death were born. Because of God's holiness, He could no longer be in the presence of the children He had created, and with sorrow in His heart He banned them from Eden and the self-fulfilling system. They no longer had access to the Kingdom of God and would live the rest of their lives in the kingdom of the world, ruled by a fallen angel named Satan. From that point, the land was cursed, and man had to toil to earn a living.

"That's all interesting, but what does it have to do with me?" Tim asked.

"Do you have a job that requires you to work long hours away from your family?"

"Yeah."

"And are you paid only a fraction of what you're worth?"

"Yeah."

"That's the curse that was placed on mankind, but did you know that you don't have to live under that curse? In fact, you don't have to toil for a living. That same self-fulfilling system is available to you today."

Tim frowned. "Now, wait a minute. Everyone has to work for a living…"

"Let's finish the story and I think your eyes will be opened."

Paul continued by explaining that when Jesus came to earth and died on the cross it wasn't just to bring salvation - the forgiveness of sins, it was to return the Kingdom of God and the self-fulfilling system, that was in Eden, back to mankind. After being baptized, receiving the Holy Spirit, and spending forty days in the desert, Jesus began preaching that the Kingdom of God was at hand. When Jesus died on the cross, he not only took all of mankind's sins – past, present, and future – but also returned rulership of the earth to man, which also returned access to the Kingdom of God and the self-fulfilling system.

Tim interrupted Paul. "Okay, now I've heard all about Jesus dying on the cross for my sins, but I don't know about all this other stuff."

"Tim, stick with me and I think it will all make sense. Galatians 3:13-14 teaches that Christ redeemed us from the curse of the Law, having become a curse for us - for it is written, cursed is everyone who hangs on a tree - in order that in Christ Jesus the blessing of Abraham might come to the Gentiles, so that we would receive the promise of the Spirit through faith. This means that Jesus took all the curses with him to the cross, including the curse on the land that caused man to have to work hard for a living. It also gave the Gentiles access to the promises of Abraham. You're not Jewish, are you?"

"No, but I'm still not understanding what this has to do with me?"

"Actually, a great deal! If you're not Jewish, then that makes you a Gentile and you now have access to the promises of Abraham through Jesus. Deuteronomy 28:1-14 describes those promises by teaching that great blessings will come upon and overtake you, if you are obedient to God. You will be blessed everywhere you go. Everything you put your hand to will be blessed and the land will be blessed. The original curse was a curse on the ground, which caused man to experience toilsome labor. The promises of Abraham removed that curse and Jesus' death on the cross gave the Gentiles access to those promises.

The Apostle Paul confirms this in Galatians 3:7 when he said, 'Understand then, that those who have faith (in Jesus) are children of Abraham.' You were grafted into Abraham's family the moment you accepted Jesus as your Savior and you now have access to the blessings. The land is no longer cursed. You are no longer required to earn a living through toilsome labor or by the sweat of your brow. Since the day Jesus died, every believer has had access to the self-fulfilling system. Knowing how to operate in it results in God prospering you without hard, stressful work."

Shaking his head, he replied, "I'm not following you. If I don't work, I can't pay my bills and we'll end up poor and homeless."

"That's exactly what Satan wants you to think. He knows that if you continue working those long, hard hours for just enough money to get by, you will never have time for a proper relationship with God, your family, or to minister to others. You and your wife will fight over money and you will struggle the rest of your life."

Tim nervously chuckled. "Yeah, you can say that again. My wife and I fight over money more than anything else."

Paul continued explaining. "The exciting part is that if you really understand and begin to implement this, the Eden system will provide what you need and you'll have the free time to develop a relationship with God, enjoy your family, and live that abundant life that Jesus promised in John 10:10."

"That all sounds good, but I don't really understand how I can apply that to my life."

"Let me tell you about some friends of mine."

Paul shared about his friend Colleen. "When I met her, Colleen was a single mom with five children working as a part-time secretary. Her husband had recently left her and due to some major medical issues, she was over a million dollars in debt. With no education beyond high school and no real marketable skills, Colleen needed a miracle. She needed the self-fulfilling system and that's exactly what she got. It arrived in the form of a network marketing business. Not having any previous network marketing, sales, or business background, Colleen could have allowed fear to destroy God's plan and keep her bound by debt, but she didn't. Now, over fourteen years later, she is completely debt free and a major contributor to her church and some non-profit organizations. She has complete time freedom to travel all over the world. Colleen is living the abundant life, because she found her self-fulfilling system in network marketing."

Next, Paul told him about Jacob, a gentleman he met in Dallas while speaking at a Christian network marketing conference.

"Jacob shared how he and his wife graduated from good colleges and secured top corporate jobs. They were both earning nice six-figure incomes and from the outside looked extremely successful. However, they worked long hours in high stress positions. Their children were being raised by strangers in a daycare center and that grieved them. Jacob felt trapped and began to pray for a solution. That solution came in the form of a network marketing business. At first Jacob wasn't interested. He felt that network marketing wasn't a legitimate business. However, after several Holy Spirit promptings, Jacob looked at the business and instantly recognized the power of residual income. Four years later, Jacob and his wife are millionaires and enjoying the total time freedom that the Eden system brings."

"Both Colleen and Jacob learned how to activate what I call the Eden Factor and are now living the lives that most people only dream about."

"The Eden Factor?"

"It's the key that gives you entrance back into Eden. I'm sure you know that Eden is no longer a place, but it is still a system that will provide for your every need, without toilsome labor. All you have to do is activate the Eden Factor and you're in."

"Okay, so how do I do that?"

"There are three activators."

Paul pulled a notepad out of his briefcase and wrote the first of three activators:

1)   Seek first the Kingdom of God

Then he continued, "God is the source of all finances, not a person's job or business or investments; it all comes from God. Matthew 6:33 says, But, seek first his kingdom and his righteousness, and all these things will be given to you as well.

The disciples, who had left their occupations to follow Jesus, were asking how they would eat, drink, and what they would wear. Jesus replied that if they would first seek the Kingdom of God and righteousness, through Jesus, that God would provide for all their needs. As time went on, that was proven in the lives of the disciples. The same is true for all believers today. By seeking the

Kingdom of God, it allows God to give each person what they need in order to live in this world."

Paul pulled out his Bible.

"Let's look at Psalm 127:1-2, because it really hammers this point home. It says, 'Unless the Lord builds the house, they labor in vain who build it…It is vain for you to rise up early, to retire late, to eat the bread of painful labors; for He gives to His beloved even in his sleep.'"

"What that is saying is that it is useless to get up early and work late – long hours every day in order to earn a living. If you let God build your business, He will give to you even when you sleep."

"Tim, how hard do you have to work for a gift?"

"Uh, well, if it's a gift, I don't have to work at all."

"Exactly! Seeking God's Kingdom first activates the Eden Factor and opens the door into that self-fulfilling system that will provide everything you need. A system that provides for your every need; doesn't that sound like residual income?"

"It sure does. This is amazing. How come I've never heard any of this?"

"I believe it's new revelation that God is unveiling for these final days on earth and we are blessed to be the recipients. Are you ready for the second activator?"

"YES!"

Paul wrote the second activator on the notepad:

2)   Meditate in the Bible

"It was through extensive study and meditation of the scriptures that God revealed the Eden Factor to me. In Joshua 1:8, it says, 'Do not let this Book of the Law depart from your mouth; meditate on it day and night, so that you may be careful to do everything written in it. Then you will be prosperous and successful.'"

"This means that you need to have the promises of God so firmly planted in your heart that they are always on your mind and coming out of your mouth. Your body will follow what you say and by becoming a doer of the Word you will enjoy success and prosperity."

"But what does it mean to meditate day and night? Does that mean I have to quit my job, become a monk and read my Bible twenty-four hours a day?"

"I struggled with that one myself," Paul said with a chuckle. "It means that we should have scriptures memorized and internalized, so that even when we don't have a Bible sitting in front of us, we can ponder the Word of God while we are showering, driving, during a break at work, or lying in bed."

"But, how does meditating in the Bible activate the Eden Factor?"

"Through faith."

"Faith?"

"Yes, faith is a key that opens the door into Eden. You gained access to God's grace by faith, when you received Jesus as your Savior. Now, you use that same faith to access the self-fulfilling system called Eden."

"So, how do I do that?"

"Well, the Bible says in Romans 10:17, Faith comes from hearing the message, and the message is heard through the word of Christ. The faith key is found by hearing the message in the Word of God. So, read your Bible out loud, listen to the Bible in your phone Bible app, and attend services and classes where the Word of God is preached, so that your mind can be renewed."

"Your mind has been programmed for years to access the world's system for making money. Now, you must retrain your mind to access the Eden Factor. One way that you do that is through daily study, meditation, and memorization of the scriptures."

"I try to read the Bible every day, but other stuff always seems to get in the way."

"I certainly understand that one. The reason that happens is that you have a very real enemy in Satan, and he doesn't want you studying and applying the Word of God, so he does everything possible to distract you. The way I conquered this was to begin each day by praying that the Lord would protect my time in the Bible by keeping the enemy away. I also asked that my ears would be deaf to the devil's words and my mind would be open to what God wanted to say through His Word."

"That worked?"

"As a matter of fact, it did and still does."

"That seems so easy. I didn't know that we could control the devil like that."

"Yes, Jesus has given all believers authority over the devil and his demons."

"So, what do you say?"

"I just say something like, 'In the powerful name of Jesus, I command that any evil spirit that is trying to hinder my time with the Lord be silenced and sent away.'"

"Wow, I don't think I could remember all that."

"The exact words aren't important. If you had a person bothering you, what would you say?

"I'd tell them to stop and leave me alone."

"Exactly. So, do the same thing with the devil and his bunch. Can you do that?"

"I believe so."

"Good. Let's move on to the third and final activator, which is seeking God's guidance through prayer. As I'm sure you know, the Holy Spirit lives in you and is your line of communication to the Father. The key is quiet times in prayer, seeking God's guidance for everything you do."

Paul wrote the final Eden Factor activator on the notepad:

3)   Seek God's Guidance Through Prayer

Once again, Paul opened his Bible and this time read from the book of Luke, chapter six and verse twelve, "One of those days Jesus went out to a mountainside to pray, and spent the night praying to God."

"How many times have you spent the whole night praying?"

"Well, uh, never."

"Me neither. Yet, here was the Son of God devoting a whole night to prayer, knowing that the following day he would be mobbed by people wanting healing, deliverance, and teaching. I don't think there is any doubt why Jesus operated with so much wisdom and power. I also figure if it's good enough for the Son of God, it certainly ought to be good enough for me and you. Oh, and you don't have to pray all night."

"Whew, that's good to hear," Tim replied, swiping a hand across his forehead.

"You still good? Do you want a break? Had enough?"

"No, this is good stuff. Keep going."

"Okay. Even though Jesus was fully God while in heaven, he had to empty himself of his godly nature and abilities in order to be born with flesh and blood. He then had to grow in wisdom and stature, just like any other man."

"There were two reasons that Jesus operated in wisdom and power. First, he knew the scriptures and second, he had developed an intimate relationship with the Father through prayer. It was during these times of prayer that Father God would give his Son insight and direction for the coming day or days. Jesus himself said in John 5:19 that he did nothing on his own, but did what he saw the Father doing. In another scripture Jesus said that he didn't say anything but what he first heard the Father say. Jesus did nothing on his own and he expected his followers to do the same."

"Father God is the Alpha and the Omega, the beginning and end. He has seen every day of your life, so doesn't it make sense to meet with Him early each day and get your marching orders?"

"Yeah, that makes a lot of sense."

"The great part is that the Father is your partner in network marketing. He wants you to be successful and will teach you how, if you just get together with Him and quietly listen. Our biggest problem in prayer is that we do all the talking and God has all the knowledge. I think that is why He gave us two ears and one mouth – He wanted us to listen twice as much as we talk. So, do what Jesus did and get alone with God in a quiet place and seek His plan for your business and life."

"Wow, I never thought of God as my business partner. I just figured He was too busy running the universe to be interested in what I was doing."

"God knew you before you were a twinkle in your parent's eyes and has counted every hair on your head. He wants to be part of everything you do, including your business. Remember that He has a plan to prosper you and it very likely includes your network marketing business, so all you have to do is get Him involved and you will prosper. Quiet time in prayer is the third and final activator for entering Eden."

"This is all so amazing. I have to admit that I was pretty down when I walked on the plane and secretly hoped that there wouldn't be anyone in the seat next to me, so I didn't have to talk, but I'm glad that you're here and shared all this with me."

"I call this a divine appointment. What are the odds that we would both end up on the same plane and sitting next to each other? It's pretty clear that God wanted us to meet and I'm beginning to see why."

Two

God's Purpose for Network Marketing

The flight attendant asked the woman next to Paul, "would you like something to drink?"

Tim had forgotten the woman was there. She looked up from her book and caught Tim's eye. He noticed that she was professional looking with short brown hair, a nicely tailored suit, and a warm smile. He returned the smile and shifted his gaze back to the attendant.

"A Diet Coke, please," the woman responded.

"A drink for you, sir?" the attendant asked Paul.

"Just some water, please."

"I'll take the same," Tim chimed in.

As the attendant rolled the cart forward, the woman in the window seat spoke for the first time.

"Sorry for eavesdropping, but I couldn't help hearing your conversation about Christianity and network marketing. I grew up going to church, but haven't attended for years and I've dabbled at times with network marketing, but have never heard anyone talk about them together."

"Actually, if you study the history of network marketing it has a similar foundation as the United States; a biblical foundation. In the early days, many people received Jesus as their Savior and Lord at network marketing meetings and conventions," Paul responded.

"I had no idea. All I've ever seen is the greed and materialism. I'm not motivated by money, so all the talk about big houses, dream cars, yachts, and such, really turned me off. By the way, my name is Susan," she said extending her hand to Paul.

"I'm Paul and this is my new friend, Tim."

"Hello Tim," she said reaching across Paul to shake Tim's hand. It was the firm handshake of a powerful and confident businesswoman.

"What do you do for a living," Paul asked Susan.

"I'm the Regional Manager for a pharmaceutical company."

"Sounds like you've done well," Paul responded.

"The only woman in middle management in my company."

"Ah, the glass ceiling."

"Yes, unfortunately I'm stuck behind the good ol' boys club and probably won't move any further."

"That's too bad. You seem quite capable."

"Thank you. That's one of the reasons I'm

interested in hearing about how Christianity and network marketing fit together. I'm fascinated by the Eden Factor you spoke of earlier, so if you don't mind me listening in, please continue."

Paul went on to describe how, contrary to the common public image, network marketing was an industry driven by service and servant leadership. No one could achieve big success in network marketing without helping other people succeed. Unlike the corporate world where it's dog-eat-dog, a network marketing leader hopes that people in his or her downline will do better than they do, because the leader earns a residual percentage of all the business in their network.

"I never looked at it that way, but I guess you're right," Susan commented. "All I've ever seen is people harassing their friends and family unmercifully until they give in and join."

"Unfortunately, that does happen, but it's not the right way to build a network marketing business. That's part of the taint in the industry."

"The taint?" Tim asked.

"As I mentioned earlier, network marketing had a biblical foundation, but then Satan got involved and began to twist things. That's why we see so much greed and materialism. It's also why we see the hard sell tactics. None of that was part of God's plan for this great industry. His intention was for it to be a vehicle that would enable His followers to enjoy the Eden Factor. That's why it's called residual income. Once you build the income, it continues whether you work the business or not."

"Fascinating," Susan commented.

"The good news is that God is beginning to redeem the network marketing industry."

"What do you mean?" asked Tim.

"Over the last few years I've noticed that many of the bad apples – distributors who were using deceptive practices – have been terminated by their company and I'm seeing many Christians rise to leadership positions where they have influence and platform."

"Why would God even care about network marketing?"

"Susan, that's a good question. God cares deeply about everything that involves His children and network marketing certainly does. I also believe that God is using this business model as one of the vehicles to transfer the wealth from the wicked to the righteous."

Paul continued by explaining what it says in Ecclesiastes 2:26. "To the man who pleases him, God gives wisdom, knowledge and happiness, but to the sinner he gives the task of gathering and storing up wealth to hand it over to the one who pleases God."

"The great wealth transfer is also referred to in Proverbs 13:12, where it says, 'A good man leaves an inheritance for his children's children, but a sinner's wealth is stored up for the righteous.' God's intention is to allow those who are willfully or inadvertently following Satan to prosper with the goal of transferring that wealth over to the righteous – those who are followers of Jesus Christ."

"Why would God do that?" Susan asked.

"The Bible talks about a great end time revival

where many people will come to know Jesus Christ as their Savior. Jesus himself said that the message of the gospel of the Kingdom would be preached to all the nations and then the end would come. As you can imagine, that's a huge task and requires a lot of money to send missionaries, beam satellite television programs, translate and print Bibles, plant churches, feed and clothe the poor, house orphans and widows, and so on. It's going to be the Christians who finance that great revival, which means God must get the money into our hands."

"That makes sense, but why network marketing?"

"God put His hand on the industry from the very beginning because it offered so much good. It's a business where people help people and one that offers financial security, free time to serve God and to raise and enjoy a family without the usual financial stresses. This is one of a very select group of business models that offers average people the opportunity for both time and financial freedom. It truly offers equal opportunity for success to anyone without regard to age, gender, race, background, intelligence, or education. There are more rags to riches stories in network marketing than any other industry."

"You make it sound so good, but it seems like more people fail than succeed."

"This is an unfortunate fact, but it's not because of a faulty business model. The primary reason people fail is because they don't work their business. That's partly due to the way the industry is conveyed – as a get rich quick scheme – which of course it's not. It's a get rich slow business, but in many cases much quicker than in traditional business," Paul responded with a chuckle.

"You said that you've done well in network marketing; what does that mean?" Susan asked.

"Yes, the Lord has blessed me abundantly and I do give Him all the credit, because when I tried to build a network marketing business on my own, it was a horrible failure. Let me put it this way. I began my business on a part-time basis and within a couple years was earning a low six-figure income. I continued building for three more years with that income building each year and then retired. I continue to support my team, but have a lot of time freedom and the company continues to deposit a large amount of money into my bank account every Friday."

"That's amazing. I've worked for the same company for nearly 20 years, putting in sixty to seventy-hour work weeks and I only earn what you did after just two years of part-time effort in network marketing. It appears that I've really missed the boat," Susan said, shaking her head.

Paul smiled. "It's never too late. I know people who have launched network marketing businesses in their sixties, seventies, and even their eighties."

"No kidding," Tim chimed in.

"It's the truth. That's the beauty of this amazing business model – anyone can be successful. Most won't, because of faulty work ethic, but everyone has the same potential to succeed," Paul said.

"Okay, I'd like to shift gears. I'm still a bit confused about this end time revival and how network marketing fits," Susan said.

"I believe that God is using network marketing in a number of ways. First, as I said earlier, God has selected it as one of the financial vehicles to transfer wealth from the wicked to the righteous. Second, network marketing is causing God's children to look more attractive to the people of the world who don't know Him. Third, those who follow Jesus as their model are givers and so God knows that if He blesses them with abundant finances, they will use the money to help others and build His Kingdom throughout the world. I know several network marketing leaders who are living on 10% and giving away 90%."

"How is that possible?" Susan asked.

"Could you live on $10,000 a month?" Paul asked.

"Very nicely," Susan responded.

"Yeah, me too," Tim added.

"Well, if you're making $100,000 a month in network marketing, and you live on 10%, that's ten grand a month. Now imagine how much good you could do by giving away $90,000 a month to those in need. Then multiply that by 10, 20, 30, or perhaps hundreds of people who will eventually get to that level of income and giving."

"Wow! Just a handful of people giving at that level could rid the world of homelessness and hunger." Susan said.

"That's exactly why God is using business systems like network marketing. Plus, network marketers know how to network, so they can more effectively spread the gospel of Jesus Christ throughout the U.S. and into other lands. The key to being part of God's plan is to recognize that no matter how good a person you are, you cannot enter God's Kingdom without being born again."

"Oh no, here comes the weird stuff," she said.

"There's nothing weird about it, Susan."

He went on to explain that because Adam and Eve were disobedient, people are all born with a sin nature, which doesn't allow them to get close to God, enter His Kingdom, or enjoy the benefits of the Eden Factor. They can try to be good enough, but it's not possible, so God created a bridge over the gulf between sin and His holiness. Out of love for all mankind, God sent His only Son to earth to live as a man and die as a sacrifice to cover the sins of mankind for all time.

People are three-part beings: Body, soul, and spirit. The body is obviously the physical body. The soul is the mind, will, and emotions. The spirit is the part of a person that was originally connected to God, but died when Adam and Eve sinned in the Garden of Eden.

When a baby is born, it means that the body and soul are born, but the spirit is still dead. However, when that child gets older and willfully accepts Jesus as his or her Savior and Lord, then the spirit is re-born and connects with God. It's like connecting cable television into a home. A person can hook their TV up to the cable outlet, but until they call the cable company and have someone activate the service, they won't be watching anything.

"That's the first time any of that has made sense. It just always seemed like a bunch of rhetoric and religious rituals that really didn't seem to have any effect on people's lives. In fact, many of the Christians I've met were more critical and had greater struggles than those who weren't Christian," Susan said.

"It's true that there are many who claim to be Christians, but they don't love people. Jesus told the disciples that people would recognize them by their love for one another. True Christians have the Spirit of God living in them and will exhibit the fruit of love."

"Now, you're getting weird on me again," she responded.

"Actually, it's wonderful. When a person acknowledges that they are a sinner and that the penalty for sin is death – both physical and spiritual - and accepts Jesus as the one and only way to spiritual re-birth and eternity with God; then the Spirit of God, referred to as the Holy Spirit enters and resides in the human spirit. The Holy Spirit then becomes our guide, counselor, and comforter. We still have our own free will and the Holy Spirit will allow us to make our own decisions – even bad ones – however He will do everything possible to direct us down the good path that results in God's blessings."

"Paul, you have a unique way of explaining things. I've always thought this talk about being born again and the Holy Spirit was way out there, but now I understand."

"Susan, have you ever accepted Jesus as your Savior and Lord?" Paul asked.

"Well, I was baptized as a child and went to

church for a number of years," she responded.

"That's good, but the Bible says that we need to make a public statement. Would you like to do that?"

"Right now? Here?"

"No time like the present. You never know when your number is going to come up and you sure don't want to die without Jesus."

"Well, I don't know. I thought you had to do that in church?"

"To God, we are the church. It's really simple. All you have to do is repeat a simple prayer and I'll lead you. The key is that you have to do it from your heart. What's your heart telling you – yes or no?"

After a few moments of silence, Susan smiled and said, "Yes."

Paul then led her in a prayer of salvation: "Father God, I know I'm a sinner headed to eternity without you. Thank you for sending your Son, Jesus, to die on the cross for my sins. Today I receive him as my Savior and commit my life to him as my Lord. Father, I receive the Holy Spirit as my guide, counselor, and comforter and look forward to serving you all the rest of my days on earth and to living with you throughout the rest of eternity. Amen."

Susan repeated after Paul and ended with "Amen".

"You have now secured a place in heaven and will live out eternity with God. You are also now an adopted daughter of God and will walk out the rest of your life with the Holy Spirit's guidance. Now, you need to know that it is only your spirit that was re-born. Your body and soul need to be renewed over time by reading and hearing the Word of God, which is the Bible. Do you have a Bible?"

"No, I've never had the need."

"I have one in my briefcase that you can have," Paul said, as he pulled the tan leather briefcase out from under the seat in front. He handed her a nice black leather Bible.

"This is a study Bible. You will find not only the scriptures, but also comments from Bible scholars about the meaning of different scriptures. You'll also find commentaries on various biblical characters, historical information, and ancient maps. I think you'll find it all very interesting."

"Thank you!", she exclaimed excitedly.

"Now we just need to get you registered in Tim's company, so that you can be a part of God's wealth transfer and enjoy total time and financial freedom."

"I guess it's time for a couple of major life decisions," she responded, with a smile.

Tim proceeded to give Susan a quick presentation, with Paul coaching him along the way. It was a great learning experience for him and in the end, she joined his company. This was far beyond anything Tim could have expected. He was starting to recognize God's hand in everything that had happened since he decided to attend the convention. He looked forward to what God would do during the balance of the flight. He intended to be a sponge and learn everything he could from Paul and now he had a new recruit who could learn right along with him. He felt very blessed.

"Now that we're all in the family, I want to share with you both about the original network marketer," Paul said.

The Original
Network Marketer

Paul proceeded to tell Tim and Susan about the original network marketer, Justin Christianson. He was conceived out of wedlock and born to a couple of teenagers. They lived under societal condemnation and in extreme poverty. Justin's father was a carpenter and although he produced excellent quality work, he was often shunned by the townspeople, keeping the family poor. An excellent student, Justin grew quickly in wisdom and knowledge, gaining the respect his father had never enjoyed.

Justin was only sixteen when his father passed away suddenly and as the oldest son, the responsibility for his mother, brothers, and sisters fell on his shoulders. Fortunately, he had learned the family trade and was a master craftsman. People traveled from far off lands to purchase his work and hear words of wisdom. Although business was good, Justin felt as if something were missing.

As time went on, Justin discovered another calling – network marketing. A friend invited him over for supper and afterwards showed Justin the business. Justin stared at the compensation plan diagram and fell in love with the concept of residual income. He joined that night and began studying everything he could find.

His sponsor taught him the fine art of networking and soon Justin had recruited twelve front-line people. Most of them were truly diamonds in the rough, so Justin devoted many hours teaching them what he had learned about networking.

Each day, Justin and his downline would go out into the common areas of town and hold a business presentation event to attract new people. Word spread quickly about the wisdom of this young man and Justin's network grew rapidly. He delivered loving messages with an authority no one had experienced before, so people flocked from miles around to hear him speak.

Justin realized that this was his true calling and so he turned the family carpentry business over to his younger brothers and began traveling from town to town, sharing his exciting life changing message and bringing new people into his network. Building leaders was one of Justin's greatest attributes and when his downline was ready, he began to send them out two by two to leverage his time and produce greater results.

The message Justin and his team were sharing reached far and wide, creating great popularity. Unfortunately, this also attracted the attention of some government regulators. They were jealous of his popularity and great wealth. In their mind it was obviously an illegal operation. They didn't even attempt to understand Justin and began to confront him on the legality of his message. They tried to trap him into making product or income claims, but Justin always operated at the highest level of integrity. This frustrated the regulators, so they began to bring false testimony against him. They figured that if the leader was gone, the team would disperse, and their troubles would be finished.

The regulators brought false claims against him and arrested Justin, placing him in jail. There he was ridiculed and beaten, as the promoter of a pyramid scheme, a heinous crime. A judge heard the case and could find no reason to sentence Justin, but the regulators persisted until finally the judge gave in. In Justin's country, the penalty for operating a pyramid scheme was death and so they executed Justin on the same day as a couple of common thieves.

With their leader gone, the team floundered for awhile, but that spark that Justin lit soon turned into a raging fire and years later Justin's team numbered in the millions. He was truly the original and greatest network marketer of all times.

"Wow, I've never heard that story before. In fact, I've never even heard his name mentioned," exclaimed Tim.

"I would have to agree with Tim," said Susan.

"That's because it's a fictional story, loosely based on the original network marketer, Jesus Christ and obviously occurred before network marketing was invented," responded Paul.

Tim slapped his forehead and said, "Well duh – a carpenter, traveling from town to town with a life changing message, I should have guessed."

"Jesus was the original network marketer and there is so much we can learn from him, about building a business. First, let's look at how Jesus built his downline," Paul said.

He continued by teaching them that Jesus initially selected a group of twelve people. These were definitely not the cream of the crop in his area; many were rough fishermen and tax collectors. This shows that the people who look good on the outside are not always the best people to recruit into a network marketing business.

"I know a top network marketer who recruited the mayor of his town and the maid who cleaned his house on the same day. He had high hopes for the mayor, who had a huge circle of influence and figured the maid would sell a few products. However, the mayor never sponsored a single person and the maid went on to build a huge business. Jesus taught us to find the people who have potential," Paul said.

"I guess that would include me," said Tim, "as I've never accomplished much."

"You are truly a diamond in the rough. A diamond starts out as a black lump of coal and when extreme pressure is applied, it turns into a precious diamond. From what you've told me, you've been under tremendous pressure. That means that God is turning you into a diamond."

Tim grinned. "I never thought of it that way."

Paul proceeded with his teaching by telling his new friends that Jesus began training the twelve and watched for his leaders to emerge. Peter, Jacob, and John showed signs of leadership and so Jesus began to meet with them separately for leadership training. God the Father, Jesus' trainer, so to speak, had taught him about leadership and so Jesus passed that on to the three emerging leaders.

Jesus recognized the importance of his message and so he held regular opportunity events that at first attracted hundreds and later thousands. At some of those gatherings he served food, so that people could focus on his message. Many joined him, but many others just couldn't understand his message and went on with their lives. Jesus knew that even if they didn't join, a seed had been planted that would one day germinate. The same is true of a network marketing business – many will hear the message, but few will join, however a seed is planted in all who hear.

"That's funny, I never thought about the times Jesus taught as opportunity events, but I suppose you're right," said Tim.

"Our opportunity events are nothing more than a chance for people to gather information, so they can make an educated decision. As it was with Jesus, our job is to present the information in a way so that those who are ready can understand the message."

"Jesus also understood the importance of

training, so he mixed in many training sessions – telling his new recruits stories that illustrated his powerful points."

"The parables!" Tim shouted, looking around sheepishly.

Paul smiled, "Yes, Jesus spoke in parables because people love stories and those who are in the looking zone are able to understand the significance of the message in each story."

"The looking zone?"

"I suppose that everyone you've presented your business to has joined, right?" he said with a smile.

"No, in fact most haven't joined."

"It's possible that some didn't join because they didn't hear what they needed, but many didn't join because they weren't at the right point in their life to be interested. They weren't in the looking zone."

"Okay, I get it. It's like the guy I met with the other day. I spoke with him a year ago and he wasn't interested, but he recently lost his job and now he is very interested."

"Exactly! That's the looking zone. Sometimes people find out they are being laid off from their job or their company is being bought out and their job is in jeopardy. Others discover a health issue. Some figure out that they aren't going to have enough money for retirement. Life changes and those changes can put people into the looking zone and that's the right time to present your business. So, stories are the key to presenting your business, because words tell, and stories sell."

"I've experienced that in my sales career," added

Susan. "If I just give people a bunch of facts, their eyes glaze over, but stories keep them attentive and interested."

"You are so right, and we need to remember that when presenting our network marketing businesses. I'll share more about presenting in a little while, but first, let's look at how Jesus prospected for his network."

Four

Jesus as a Prospector

Prospecting . . . ugh! Tim thought. He was remembering the many conversations with friends, family members, co-workers, people from church, and strangers. Nearly all of them had in one way or another called him crazy for being involved in that kind of business. His parents were the worst. They had always supported his career choices, so he was surprised when they reacted so negatively to the network marketing business. They told him he was involved in an illegal pyramid scheme and wouldn't have anything to do with it. His heartbeat quickened, as he thought of that conversation, one of the worst ever with his parents. Yet, he knew that prospecting was a critical part of success in network marketing.

"Jesus was the greatest prospector of all time and we can learn a great deal by studying his methods," Paul said.

"It's strange thinking about the Son of God as a prospector," Tim commented.

"Is it proper to reduce him to that level?" Susan asked.

"Yes, Jesus was the Son of God. He was also the Son of Man, which was the way he most often referred to himself. As we study Jesus, we'll find that he was a prospector, presenter, trainer, and leader, all things that you must become excellent at, if you want to be successful in network marketing."

"I suppose you're right," Tim said. "I've just had a real hard time with prospecting. Mostly people just think I'm crazy or I'm involved in something illegal. Prospecting has become kind of a bad word to me."

"I can certainly relate. There was a time early in my network marketing career when I felt the same way. When I started, I contacted over 100 of my best prospects and all but one said no. The worst part was that they didn't just say no, they had to give me advice or they just wouldn't return my calls."

"Yeah, that's what happened to me," Tim replied. "So, how did you get beyond that?"

"That's a good question. First, I had to recognize that not everyone was at the right time in their life for network marketing. Second, I began to think of it as sifting for diamonds. I was once told that prospecting was like being on a small sandy beach where many diamonds had been previously buried.

All I had to do was sift through all the sand in order to find the diamonds. Some of the diamonds were big, representing a person who would build a huge network and others were small, representing the person who might only recruit a hand full of people. The key was that I knew the diamonds were there, so I wasn't concerned about the sand, which represented all the people who weren't interested."

"Wow, that's an amazing example," said Tim. "I never thought about prospecting in that way."

"There is another key to prospecting and that is that you have to become a master prospector. In other words, you need to work at it until you have an excellent and proven approach. It's one thing to prospect a lot of people and something else to sponsor a lot of people. I know many top network marketing leaders who don't prospect very many people, but they have huge networks."

"How is that possible?" Susan inquired.

"They sponsor leaders. It's unfortunate that the industry has often taught people to sponsor anyone who can fog a mirror, when in reality we should treat prospecting like an interview process. If you were the President of a major corporation with the need for a new Vice President, you wouldn't just go out on the street and start asking people if they needed a job, would you?"

"No way," said Tim.

"Absolutely not," responded Susan.

"Well, then why would you do that in network marketing?"

"Huh?" Tim said.

"One of the secrets to network marketing success

is to prospect and sponsor leaders. As you go through your life, you'll find them in leadership roles, supervising teams of people. It might be the bank manager or the shift manager at the local fast food restaurant. You'll find them in major corporations, non-profit organizations, teaching at schools, sweeping the floors after hours, and running their own businesses. A leader is easy to recognize, because he or she has people who trust them. Think about the people in your lives . . . whose name pops up?"

"Pete," said Tim.

"Linda," added Susan.

"Tell me about Pete," said Paul.

"Well, he's the branch manager for an insurance company in our town."

"What's he like?"

"Well, he's a real take charge kind of guy. Sort of intimidates me at times."

"I'll bet that you haven't talked with him about your business."

"Well, uh, I've meant to, does that count?" he said, with a sheepish grin.

"Susan, tell me about Linda."

"She's been my best friend for over twenty years and is the regional manager for a franchise operation. Like Pete, she's a real take charge person."

"There you go. You've each identified a person in your life who would likely make an excellent addition to your network marketing business. However, the key is going to be whether they are in the looking zone and that was one of Jesus' strengths as a prospector. He could tell when people were ready for a change."

"He was the Son of God, of course he would know when they were ready," Tim blurted.

"He's right," Susan chimed in.

"You bring up a good point. So many people think that Jesus was able to do the things he did, because he was God in flesh. Yes, Jesus was fully God, but he emptied himself of his godly attributes in order to be fully man. He had to be fully man in order to be a legal sacrifice for the sins of all mankind. So, from birth to death, Jesus operated just as you and I would. In fact, Jesus told his followers that he did nothing on his own, only what he had first seen the Father do and he said nothing, except what he had heard the Father say. Jesus had to tap into God the same way we do."

"Then how did he turn water into wine, multiply the fishes and loaves, and heal people?" Tim asked.

"He didn't do any of those things. Rather his faith moved the hand of the Father to do those things. That's why after a person was healed, he would often say that their faith had healed them. He also taught in Matthew 17:20 that if you have faith the size of a mustard seed that nothing will be impossible for you. Then in John 14:12 he said, "I tell you the truth, anyone who has faith in me will do what I have been doing. He will do even greater things than these, because I am going to the Father.""

"So, what you're saying is that if we have enough faith, we could do the things Jesus did?" Susan asked.

"It's not what I said; rather it's what Jesus said,"

Paul replied, with a smile.

"Wow, I never knew that," Tim said.

"That's why so many Christian network marketers struggle, because they don't understand the authority they walk in and how powerful faith can be."

"Okay, so what does all this have to do with prospecting?" Tim interjected.

Paul chuckled. "I suppose I did take us off on a bit of a rabbit trail, didn't I? However, it was important for you to understand that you have untapped power and abilities that you can use to build your business. If you take the time each day to pray and ask God for guidance, wisdom, favor, and knowledge, He will give them to you. Then people will pop into your mind or you'll have a sense that someone is ready for your business. It will reduce the number of rejections and you'll see many more successes."

"I'm all for that."

"Okay, so the first key to Jesus' ability to prospect was that he never did anything without first seeking the Father's guidance. It was the Father who told Jesus who to speak with, who to heal, who to raise from the dead. It was the Father who turned water into wine, multiplied the fishes and loaves, and put the coin in the fish's mouth. But, it was Jesus' faith that allowed all that to work. God works through our faith in everything. Now I want to turn your attention to his method of prospecting," Paul said.

Tim pulled out a pad and pen. "Okay, I'm ready."

Paul continued, "In Matthew 4, verses 18-20, we see Jesus approach a couple of fishermen, Simon and his brother Andrew. These were Jesus' first prospects. He said to them, "Follow me and I will make you fishers of men." They immediately dropped their nets and followed Jesus. Why do you think they were willing to give up their livelihood to follow Jesus?"

"Because he was the Son of God," Tim blurted.

"A moment ago, we established that Jesus set aside his godly attributes in order to become a flesh man, so this was the flesh man that Simon and Andrew were responding to."

"Was it because Jesus had already sought the Father and knew that Simon and Andrew were ready?" Susan asked.

"Bingo! Right on the mark. Just as with each of us, Jesus had the Holy Spirit living in him and that was his connection with the Father. Although the Bible doesn't say it, I believe that the Father had already prepared Simon and Andrew and that He then told Jesus the exact words to speak to them."

"So, if we translate that over to network marketing, God is preparing people we know or will encounter and if we're communicating with Him in prayer, He'll give us the right words to speak to those people," Susan said.

"You're catching on quickly. You see we go out on our own and start talking with people, when most of them aren't in the looking zone. However, God knows who is ready, will prepare those people, and then give you the exact words they need to hear in order to be interested. All you have to do is tap into what your business partner, God, is doing and you're assured of prospecting success."

"Wow, it seems like there should be more to it. Don't we need to learn some sales or prospecting techniques? Tim asked.

"Those are all worldly ways of prospecting and there is nothing wrong with knowing those things, but they aren't going to do you a bit of good, if you aren't seeking God for who to speak with or how to get the word out. If you seek God for your prospecting methods, He will tell you to mail letters or e-mails to a certain list and will even give instruction on what message to write. If you look at your prospect list, God will tell you who to call and what to say. If you're out in the world among groups of people and have sought God, He will tell you who to speak with and give you the words. All you have to do is be bold enough to walk up and open your mouth or pick up the phone and call."

"So, we don't have to memorize any scripts or have power closes ready?"

"Again, there is nothing wrong with those things and they will definitely help with your confidence, but if you're completely in tune with God, then He will give you the right words. The exact words the prospect needs to hear."

"I'm really beginning to understand how this works," Susan said. "It's strange, because I've felt that I should speak with that man across the aisle and what you've said just confirms my inclination."

"Good for you," Paul said, as he moved to let her out.

"Wow, she just joined and she's prospecting

someone. I don't know if I could do that."

"On your own, your right, but with God all things are possible. You've just got to learn to lean on God more. Proverbs 3:5 says, "Trust in the LORD with all your heart and lean not on your own understanding." The more you trust in the Lord, the bolder you will be and the bigger your business will grow."

"I've grown up having to trust in myself so much that it's been hard to trust in God. I've had so many people let me down that it's hardened me. I need to learn to let the walls down and trust again,"

"God is easy to trust, because He's always faithful."

"He is, isn't He?" Tim whispered.

Just then, Susan returned to her seat with a huge smile.

"What happened?" Tim asked.

"You won't believe this. His name is Gordon and he's a Vice President with a large high-tech company. Unfortunately, Gordon is coming back from a meeting where it was announced that his company was purchased, and his job eliminated. He did receive a six-month severance package and get this he's been praying for God to open a door and reveal the next stage of his life. He's very interested and wants to know more. I got all his pertinent information and promised to call him when I got back home."

"There you go. When you listen for God and are obedient, He will lead you to the people who are in the looking zone. Good job!"

"How come God did that with Susan, but not

with me?"

"She's a brand-new Christian, so she's less jaded and more in tune with God. You're going to have to break through some paradigms that you've built up over the years, before you can clearly hear the Lord. The great part is that with God those things will break off quickly, if you're ready to release them."

"Oh, yeah, I'm ready to get rid of anything that would keep me from hearing God."

"Then, all you have to do is release those paradigms to God and tell Him you want to hear more clearly."

Paul led Tim in a quick prayer that God would show Tim what paradigms are holding him back and how to release them. Susan joined in quietly.

"So, let's review Jesus as prospector. First, he was completely in tune with God and sought Him every day in every way. Second, he was willing to take steps of faith by walking up to people. Third, Jesus allowed Father God, through the Holy Spirit, to speak through him. He never tried to do or say anything on his own, but rather trusted completely in God for everything. If you begin to model Jesus in this way, you will be amazed at the results. It's a major reason why I've been so successful."

"I'm in," Tim said.

"Me too," added Susan.

"Good, then let's move on and talk about Jesus as a presenter."

Five

Jesus as a Presenter

Paul started with a question. "In my thirty years of network marketing experience, I've noticed a commonality among the top income earners, any idea what that might be?"

"They're outgoing and can talk with anyone?" Tim answered.

"That's true, but not quite what I'm looking for."

"Could it be that they're excellent presenters," Susan responded.

"That's also true, though not exactly the correct answer, but you're on the right track. All the top money earners have been excellent at telling stories."

"Words tell and stories sell," Susan added.

"Absolutely correct and Jesus was the best

storyteller of all times. Let's look at a few of his stories, which are referred to in the Bible as parables."

"Yeah, that's always confused me. Why do they call them parables?", Tim asked.

"Good question. The word parable is derived from the Greek verb paraballo. That word is composed from two words. The first is para, which means beside. The second is ballo, which means to cast. So, put those two together and you get the casting of a story with a comparison of two things side-by-side for the purpose of teaching a lesson. Let's look at a couple of Jesus' parables and this will make more sense."

Paul opened his Bible and read Matthew 13:44, "The kingdom of heaven is like treasure hidden in a field. When a man found it, he hid it again, and then in his joy went and sold all he had and bought that field."

Closing the Bible, he began to explain the parable.

"This parable is a comparison of something spiritual and something in the physical world, which Jesus did often to help people understand how things worked in the spirit realm. In this particular parable Jesus taught how to get into the Kingdom of heaven based on something that any listener would understand – finding a hidden treasure."

He continued by sharing that if someone were walking through a vacant lot and stumbled across a buried treasure, they would quickly find the owner of the lot and do whatever they could to purchase the land. Once they purchased the land, they would also have ownership of the treasure. Well, the kingdom of heaven is worth more than any earthly treasure, because it ensures an eternal life with God in heaven. Jesus gave up his life, so that all people could have access to the treasure by giving up their sinful ways and committing their lives to God.

He then motioned to Susan, "Just as you did earlier, all a person has to do is repent of their sins and recognize that Jesus is their Savior and the only way to the Father in heaven. By accepting Jesus as their Savior and Lord, they receive a great treasure now in the Holy Spirit and an even greater treasure later, eternity with God."

"I've read that scripture a hundred times and never fully understood it until now," Tim replied.

"Now, let's go back a few verses and look at the parable of the weeds in Matthew 13:24-30," Paul said, opening his Bible once again.

He shared with them this parable, "The kingdom of heaven is like a man who sowed good seed in his field. But while everyone was sleeping, his enemy came and sowed weeds among the wheat, and went away. When the wheat sprouted and formed heads, then the weeds also appeared. The owner's servants came to him and said, 'Sir, didn't you sow good seed in your field? Where then did the weeds come from?' 'An enemy did this,' he replied. The servants asked him, 'Do you want us to go and pull them up?' 'No,' he answered, 'because while you are pulling the weeds, you may root up the wheat with them. Let both grow together until the harvest. At that time, I will tell the harvesters: First collect the weeds and tie them in bundles to be burned;

then gather the wheat and bring it into my barn.'"

He continued by explaining that this parable speaks of the end times, when Jesus returns to reclaim the earth. At that time there will be righteous people, those who have accepted Jesus as their Savior and Lord, and what the Bible refers to as wicked people, those who have not accepted Jesus. In the parable, the wheat represents the righteous and the weeds are the wicked. Because people have been given free will and the opportunity to choose God or the world, heaven or hell, God will allow the wicked to live alongside the righteous until the end. At that time, which is referred to as the harvest, Jesus will send angels to separate the weeds from the wheat. The weeds will then be thrown into the fiery pit, which was created for Satan and his fallen angels, but will now be the eternal home for those who rebel against God by not receiving Jesus as their Savior. The wheat or the righteous people, will be gathered and enter heaven to spend eternity with God.

"Can you see how Jesus is using something from the natural world, that the people of that time would easily recognize, in order to show them the spiritual side?" Paul asked.

"Yes," replied Susan.

"I sure can," said Tim.

"Good, then let's look at one more, which is my favorite parable." Paul opened his Bible to Matthew 25:14-28. "This is the parable of the loaned money; better known as the parable of the talents."

"Yeah, I love this one!" Tim responded.

Paul proceeded to read the parable out loud, as

they both leaned in, listening intently to every word. "Again, it will be like a man going on a journey, who called his servants and entrusted his property to them. To one he gave five talents of money, to another two talents, and to another one talent, each according to his ability. Then he went on his journey. The man who had received the five talents went at once and put his money to work and gained five more. So also, the one with the two talents gained two more. But the man who had received the one talent went off, dug a hole in the ground and hid his master's money.

"After a long time, the master of those servants returned and settled accounts with them. The man who had received the five talents presented the master with 10 talents. 'Master,' he said, 'you entrusted me with five talents. See, I have gained five more.' His master replied, 'Well done, good and faithful servant! You have been faithful with a few things; I will put you in charge of many things. Come and share your master's happiness!'"

"The man with the two talents also came. 'Master,' he said, 'you entrusted me with two talents; see, I have gained two more.' His master replied, 'Well done, good and faithful servant! You have been faithful with a few things; I will put you in charge of many things. Come and share your master's happiness!'"

"Then the man who had received the one talent came. 'Master,' he said, 'I knew that you are a hard man, harvesting where you have not sown and gathering where you have not scattered seed. So, I was afraid and went out and hid your talent in the ground. See, here is what belongs to you.' His master replied, 'You wicked, lazy servant! You knew that I harvest where I have not sown and gather where I have not scattered seed? Well then, you should have put my money on deposit with the bankers, so that when I returned, I would have received it back with interest. Take the talent from him and give it to the one who has the ten talents.'"

Paul continued by explaining that this story taught several lessons. First, the master represents Jesus who has gone away and left stewardship of the world to mankind. Jesus will one day return, and every person will have to give an accounting of how well they handled what God gave them – money, abilities, relationships, and time. The second lesson to be learned is that God provides money to people according to their ability to handle it. If they properly use what He has given them, then they are rewarded with more. However, if they don't use the money to create an increase for the Kingdom of God, then even what they have will be taken away and given to those who have used money properly.

"That kind of sounds like the wealth transfer you were talking about earlier. Is it?" Susan asked.

"You are very astute. Yes, Jesus was teaching that if people use their money for personal reasons only and never use it to bring increase to the Kingdom of God, what they have will be taken away and given to someone who will."

"So, what do you mean by bringing an increase to the Kingdom of God?"

"When you tithe or give money to the church, it is used to provide a place where the poor can be served. Whether it's food or clothing or spiritual food in the way of teaching from the Bible, it's all creating an increase in the Kingdom of God. Also, when you give money to missionaries or ministries that are taking the gospel of Jesus Christ throughout the United States and into the far corners of the world, you are causing increase in the Kingdom of God. Anytime, you give money that helps the poor and causes people to hear about Jesus, accept him, and become his disciples, you are doing something good with your money and God will reward you."

"That's exciting, but again, how does all this apply to network marketing?" Tim asked.

"Always right to the point," Paul said, with a smile. "Okay, let's pull it all together. The key here is that in order to be a great network marketing presenter, you must be like Jesus and tell stories that will help people relate and understand. Tim, give me a nutshell outline of your network marketing presentation."

"Well, uh, I first tell them about the history of the network marketing industry and how it has grown through the years. Next, I share the history of my company and some growth statistics. Then I go over the entire product line. That's followed by a detailed description of the compensation plan. I end by covering how to get started and the training procedure."

"How long does that usually take?"

"About two hours."

"How do your prospects respond?"

"Well, they listen intently through the first hour or so and then I seem to lose them. I think it's something about that spot in the presentation that I need to fix."

"Although there are several things that need to be fixed, that isn't why you're losing them. It's because your presentation is too long and you're just telling them. Remember what Susan said, 'words tell, and stories sell.' Let me give you another version of that, facts tell, and stories sell. You need to include more stories in your presentation, and you'll keep their attention."

"I had never thought about that, but it sure makes sense. Thanks!"

"You're welcome. You see Jesus understood this principle, which is why he very rarely ever taught without telling a story or parable. We should learn from his example and use stories to deliver key points, rather than facts and figures. Now, don't get me wrong, there are places for the facts and figures, but stories will always produce better results."

"In my sales job, I have all kinds of stories I've amassed through the years, but how do I use stories in network marketing if I don't have any?" Susan asked.

"You use other people's stories. I'm sure that there are probably many great stories within the company you've just joined, and Tim can help you with that. Also, there are plenty of stories you'll find on CDs, videos, DVDs, and websites. You can use stories to share why the industry and your company are so great. Share stories about the products and how they're impacting people's lives. However, be careful in this area, as the government regulators are really clamping down on personal testimonies, particularly as they relate to nutritional supplements and the impact on disease. Also, be careful with income claims. Check with your company's compliance department to see what you can and can't say. However, don't let that stop you from telling stories."

"Alright, so telling stories is a key to being a good presenter, what else?" Tim asked.

"In answer to that question, let's go back into the Bible and study a situation. Let's look at Matthew 16:13–20."

Paul began to read, "When Jesus came to the region of Caesarea Philippi, he asked his disciples, 'Who do people say the Son of Man is?' They replied, 'Some say John the Baptist; others say Elijah; and still others, Jeremiah or one of the prophets.' 'But what about you?' he asked. 'Who do you say I am?' Simon Peter answered, 'You are the Christ, the Son of the living God.'"

"Jesus replied, 'Blessed are you, Simon son of Jonah, for this was not revealed to you by man, but by my Father in heaven. And I tell you that you are Peter, and on this rock, I will build my church, and the gates of Hades will not overcome it. I will give you the keys of the kingdom of heaven; whatever you bind on earth will be bound in heaven, and whatever you loose on earth will be loosed in heaven.' Then he warned his disciples not to tell anyone that he was the Christ."

He then explained that Jesus was presenting several messages. First that he was truly the Son of God. Second, that Peter had answered not by his own wisdom, but rather by wisdom given to him by

Father God. Finally, Jesus taught them that whatever they bind or forbid or don't allow on earth, God will enforce in heaven and whatever they loose or release or allow on earth, God will allow in heaven.

Satan, the fallen angel and his minions are always trying to stop the work of God by destroying mankind. When a born-again believer, in prayer, binds or stops something, then God sends His angels to make sure that Satan and his forces of darkness are stopped and if that person looses or releases something through prayer, God sends angels to help it happen. Since every born-again believer has the Holy Spirit living inside, all of this is guided by the Spirit of God and thus is within His will.

"That's great, but I'm still not understanding how this relates to presenting," Tim blurted.

"It has everything to do with presenting. Tell me what you see Jesus doing in the passage I just read."

"He's asking questions."

"Bullseye! Right on the mark. Jesus was a master at involving his audience through questions. Often, they were thought provoking questions that required more than a simple yes or no answer. That is something you must learn in order to be successful in network marketing. In fact, you should rarely make a statement that doesn't end with a question; particularly if you're doing a one-on-one presentation."

"What do you mean by that?"

"I think I know the answer," Susan interjected.

"Go ahead," Paul responded.

"For example, if I said that my product would help increase efficiency and showed the prospect some studies to prove my point, I would end the statement with a question like, 'can you see how that would be beneficial to your company?'"

"Ding! Ding! Ding! You win the prize," Paul said. "The question forces the prospect to get involved. So, Tim can you think of a statement and question that would fit your company."

"Well, uhhh, yeah I guess so. If I could see that a person was overweight and mentioned that one of my products has been proven in clinical trials to help people lose weight, I might ask if that would be something that would interest them."

"That's certainly a possibility, but given their situation, it might also offend them. So, a better question would be 'can you see how that might benefit some people you know?'"

"Ah, gotcha, that makes sense."

"So, let's recap what we've learned so far. Jesus told stories that captured people's attention and helped them understand more complicated topics by relating them to something simple and common. He involved his audience by asking questions; often thought-provoking questions, which helped him maintain control of the presentation and determined whether his listeners were understanding. Next, let's examine what Jesus did when someone didn't understand."

Paul opened his Bible to Mark 4:3-9 and read the passage which told the parable of the four soils. When Jesus realized that his disciples weren't understanding the parable, he explained it in terms they could understand.

"As a presenter, it is our responsibility to make sure that people understand. We need to do this by asking questions. When they don't understand, we should, as Jesus did, stay patient and explain it using different terms," Paul said.

"That's an area I need to work on," commented Susan. "When people don't understand what I'm saying, I quite often get upset and say things I shouldn't."

"Galatians 5:22 lists patience or long-suffering as a fruit of the spirit. Fortunately, it is part of God's character or He would have zapped all of us long ago. It's also part of the character that the Holy Spirit is helping us build, so that we can accomplish God's plan for our lives."

"So, is that it?" Tim asked.

"No, there's one more aspect of the way that Jesus presented that I want us to examine. This can be found in Mark 1:15 when Jesus said, 'The time has come. The Kingdom of God is near. Repent and believe the good news!' So, what can we learn about presenting from this short message?"

"Wow, I have no idea."

"I'm baffled, as well," Susan added.

"Presentations should always end with a call to action. Here we see Jesus explaining the timing, what is happening, and what they should do. When you present your network marketing business, your presentations should always tell prospects what to do next. Do you want them to go to a website and get more information? Join your business? Purchase some products or utilize a service? It's important for you to direct them to the next step. Does that make sense?"

"Absolutely," Susan said.

"What about you, Tim?"

"Oh, sorry I was thinking about what Jesus said, 'the Kingdom of God is near.' That fits with the Eden Factor you were talking about earlier, doesn't it?"

"It sure does. Jesus came to return dominion over Eden, which is the Kingdom of God here on earth, to mankind. You're very astute. I'm glad you recognized that!

"Did you have any thoughts about presentations?"

"I'm sorry, I didn't really catch that either. Would you share that again?"

"No worries. Jesus presented information and then called people to action. When you give a business presentation, it's critical that you clearly present the prospect's next step – more information, join your business, or purchase your products. By giving them a call to action, you maintain control of the presentation and direct them to a positive outcome."

"That makes sense."

"Okay, would one of you like to give me the four keys to an effective presentation that we learned from Jesus?"

"Can I give it a shot?" Tim asked.

"Shoot," Paul replied.

"We're to tell stories, because words or facts tell and stories sell," Tim began.

"Good. What else?"

"We should involve prospects by asking questions."

"Excellent! What type of questions?"

"Uh, let me see . . . Oh yeah, thought provoking questions."

"You're on a roll. What's next?"

"It's our responsibility to make sure the prospect understands by asking confirming questions. If they aren't catching on, then we should explain in a different way, using different language."

"You're the man! Okay, one more."

"Call people to action. Give them a next step toward a positive result."

"You've got it! How about you, Susan, are you tracking with us?"

"It's all making sense to me and I can't wait to start using what I'm learning."

Motioning to Gordon across the aisle, Paul said, "It appears that you'll get that opportunity very soon. Okay, how about shifting gears and talking about Jesus as a trainer?"

They both nodded in agreement.

Jesus as a Trainer

The flight attendant arrived with food just as Paul was beginning to teach Susan and Tim about Jesus as a trainer.

"It appears that perhaps the Lord wants us to take a break and eat," Paul said.

"I don't know about you two, but I'm starved," Tim replied.

"Now that I think about it, I am hungry," Susan added.

"Father God, we thank you for this day and for this food which you have provided. Thank you for this divine appointment and for new friends. We look forward to seeing your plan unfold in our lives. Bless the food to our bodies and keep us safe during the balance of this flight. In Jesus name we pray.

Amen." Paul prayed.

"Amen," they both said in unison.

"Not bad for airplane food," Tim said, after a few bites.

"I've certainly had worse," Susan replied.

As they were eating, Tim began daydreaming. For the first time in many months, he was excited about the future. He smiled at the thought of standing on stage at next year's convention, receiving an award for top performance. He continued to imagine a large group of his downline letting out a huge roar as he shook the President's hand as a photographer snapped a picture. In his imagination, he could see his wife in the first row, grinning ear-to-ear. It felt good.

It was at that moment that Tim heard a voice in his mind. *You know that's just a pipe dream. You'll never be on stage. You're a loser. You've always been a loser and you'll always be a loser. Why don't you just give up on this stupid business and go get a real job.* Strangely the voice sounded like his father. He cringed at the thought. His father had been so critical of network marketing and had said similar things.

His stomach tightened as the convention scene disappeared. It was replaced by an image of himself with a full head of gray hair, hunched over a desk. *Dozing again?* The voice startled him. It was a different voice . . . sounding like his boss. *I know you've been with the company for a long time, but that doesn't give you the right to sleep on the job. Get to work. Remember that report has a 2:00 deadline.* In the vision, Tim sighed and began typing. Pain shot through his fingers. He sighed again, deeper this time.

"Tim, are you all right?" Paul said.

"Uh, yeah, why?"

"Well, you were shaking your head and rubbing your fingers."

"Oh, just a daymare."

"A daymare?" Susan asked.

"You know, like a nightmare only during the day," he said, with a sheepish grin.

"What were you thinking about?" Susan asked.

"Oh, nothing important."

"Come on, Tim, we're all friends here," Paul prodded.

"Well, first I was thinking about receiving an award on stage at the convention next year."

"That doesn't sound bad," Paul responded.

"That part was great, but then I heard this voice, that sounded like my Dad, telling me that I was a loser. The scene changed to me as an old man, slaving over a computer with a tyrant for a boss who sounded like my boss."

"That is a daymare," Susan said.

"The voices may have sounded like your Dad or boss, but it was really Satan. He likes to masquerade as people in our life. John 10:10 says that the thief comes only to steal, kill, and destroy. The thief is Satan and he was just trying to steal the dream that God had given you. Hold on to that first vision, because it's likely that God was showing you a glimpse of the future. Remember that God has a plan to prosper you and not to harm you, so clearly the first part of your daydream was from

God," Paul said.

"How do I keep Satan from getting to me like that?"

"The apostle Paul said that we should take every thought captive and make it obedient to Christ. In other words, compare it to the Word of God and if it doesn't match up with the promises of God, then reject it. When a thought comes into my head that is suspect, I first compare it to the Bible and if it's clearly not from God, I actually grab it out of the air with my hand and toss it away. That seems to help me. Perhaps it will help you too."

"That's great, I love it!" he said, grabbing something out of the air and tossing it to the back of the plane, while making an explosion sound.

After handing his trash to the flight attendant, Paul said, "Okay, would you two like to hear about Jesus as a trainer?"

"Yes," Susan responded.

"Yeah, me too," Tim added.

"As you can probably imagine, Jesus was the best trainer of all time. In fact, he trained his disciples so well that they went on, even in the face of life-threatening persecution, and built a huge network that spans the world."

Paul continued by sharing that Jesus was a multi-faceted trainer. At times he would use a lecture format, during which he spoke and didn't solicit input from his audience. He opened his Bible and read Luke 16:19-31, "There was a rich man who was dressed in purple and fine linen and lived in luxury every day. At his gate was laid a beggar named Lazarus, covered with sores and longing to eat what fell from the rich man's table. Even the dogs came and licked his sores. The time came when the beggar died, and the angels carried him to Abraham's side. The rich man also died and was buried. In hell, where he was in torment, he looked up and saw Abraham far away, with Lazarus by his side. So he called to him, 'Father Abraham, have pity on me and send Lazarus to dip the tip of his finger in water and cool my tongue, because I am in agony in this fire.' But Abraham replied, 'Son, remember that in your lifetime you received your good things, while Lazarus received bad things, but now he is comforted here, and you are in agony. And besides all this, between us and you a great chasm has been fixed, so that those who want to go from here to you cannot, nor can anyone cross over from there to us.' He answered, 'Then I beg you, father, send Lazarus to my father's house, for I have five brothers. Let him warn them, so that they will not also come to this place of torment.' Abraham replied, 'They have Moses and the Prophets; let them listen to them.' 'No, father Abraham,' he said, 'but if someone from the dead goes to them, they will repent.' He said to him, 'If they do not listen to Moses and the Prophets, they will not be convinced even if someone rises from the dead.'"

"This is a great example of Jesus using a lecture style of training. Jesus wanted to teach them several lessons at the same time and so the lecture style was most effective."

"I'm really confused," Susan replied. "You've talked about how God wants us prosperous and yet in this scripture the rich man goes to hell and the poor man goes to heaven. Am I misunderstanding what Jesus was teaching?"

"That is a bit confusing. However, as you see in the scripture, the rich man did not use his money to take care of the poor and the Bible makes it very clear that when God blesses us with wealth, we are to use it properly by taking care of those less fortunate. Lazarus, which by the way isn't the same Lazarus that Jesus raised from the dead, was a poor beggar, but obviously he was devoted to God or he would not have gone to heaven."

"That makes more sense."

"Good. Now, there will be times when you too need to pass on information to your downline and the lecture mode is a good way to do it. However, you must make sure that you don't do your entire training presentation as a lecture, as you'll lose your downline's attention. You should lecture for no more than ten to fifteen minutes at a time and then shift into a different method."

"Yeah, I remember those boring lectures in high school and college," Tim replied.

"That's why you also see Jesus using stories. We talked about that earlier. What's the saying that we need to remember?"

"Facts tell and stories sell," Tim blurted.

"Good. Mixing stories in with your trainings will help keep your downline interested and focused. You can use product testimonies when training about products, but what do we need to remember?"

"Not to make any health claims that could get us and the company in trouble," Susan said.

"Excellent! When discussing the business side,

you can give a couple of business stories, but again there is something we need to remember not to do.

"No income claims!" Tim exclaimed.

"Very good. I'm impressed with your retention."

"We have a good teacher."

"Yes, we do, and his name is Jesus," Paul said, winking at Tim and continuing, "Along with stories, Jesus used a lot of word pictures to help his disciples gain deeper understanding through association."

Paul thumbed through the pages of his Bible and read John 15:1-6, "I am the true vine, and my Father is the gardener. He cuts off every branch in me that bears no fruit, while every branch that does bear fruit, he prunes so that it will be even more fruitful. You are already clean because of the word I have spoken to you. Remain in me, and I will remain in you. No branch can bear fruit by itself; it must remain in the vine. Neither can you bear fruit unless you remain in me. I am the vine; you are the branches. If a man remains in me and I in him, he will bear much fruit; apart from me you can do nothing. If anyone does not remain in me, he is like a branch that is thrown away and withers; such branches are picked up, thrown into the fire and burned."

He looked up from his Bible and continued. "This is a great word picture that shows us the proper relationship with Jesus. At the time that Jesus walked the earth, it was an agricultural-based society, so many of his examples were as such. Here Jesus compares himself to a vine that is coming off a tree. The tree would be Father God and then Jesus the vine and then we are the branches. Just as with real branches, if they are cut away from the vine, they will whither and die. If we are away from God and not receiving His life-giving Word for even just a short time, we too will whither and die, spiritually."

"That's a great illustration," Susan said.

"Jesus was a master trainer and both of you can be as well, but it takes time and work. Think about your business and what you could use to illustrate different parts of it. For example, you could describe network marketing by comparing it to someone telling you about a great movie, book, or restaurant. You could compare the residual income you earn to the royalties earned by a book author or a musician who produces top selling recordings. You could compare your nutritional supplements to car insurance – you can't see them in action, but they're always protecting you."

Paul noticed that Tim was writing furiously. "Am I going too fast for you?"

"No, keep it coming, this is great stuff!"

"Jesus also mixed questions into his trainings to keep his followers on their toes. For example, as he was preparing to teach about God's multiplication system in Mark 8:5, he asked how many loaves of bread they had. This question was used to gather information which could be used in the training presentation. He then went on to give thanks and the bread was multiplied to feed a group of somewhere between ten and fifteen thousand people."

"Do you think that really happened or is it just one of those stories that got exaggerated through the years?" Tim asked.

"I believe that the Bible was written by man, but completely inspired by God. That means that there can't be anything in the Bible that isn't the absolute truth, or it would negate the whole book. You might find it interesting that man has spent thousands of years trying to disprove the Bible, yet not one thing has ever been proven incorrect. In fact, science and archaeology continue to prove the Bible to be inerrant."

"So, the point you're making is that it's fine to ask questions during a training to gather information which can be used later in the presentation, is that correct?" Susan asked.

"That's correct. Jesus also used questions to seek feedback. We can find an example of this in Mark 8:21, where Jesus used a question to check on their understanding of what he had just presented. As you train, it's always good to add a question such as 'did that make sense?' or 'can you see how that works?' just to make sure your downline is still tracking with you. Questions will keep them from drifting off into daydreams."

Paul continued, "Finally, Jesus trained by modeling. He went out to the people, instead of sitting in the synagogue waiting for people to show up. He taught the disciples about compassion, by being compassionate. A great example is in Luke 12 when Jesus reached out to touch a leper in order to heal him. In those days, to touch a leper was sure death, so it showed Jesus' disciples two things; first was his authority and second his compassion for the man. He could just as easily have spoken the healing into existence."

"I've always wondered why Jesus touched the guy," Tim said.

"The leper hadn't been touched for many years and that one simple act of compassion probably opened him spiritually to receive the healing," he said and then continued talking about how Jesus modeled his training subjects.

"Other examples of training through modeling were the many times Jesus went off alone to pray. He was teaching his followers the importance of receiving wisdom and direction from the Father, by having quiet time with Him. As you begin to train your downline, remember to model for them. Show them how to prospect over the phone by having them listen to your calls. Take them when you go out in public, so they can hear what you say to people and view your presentations. They need to see you doing the things you are telling them to do in order for your trainings to carry power."

"This is such great stuff," Tim commented, still furiously taking notes.

"Absolutely," Susan added.

"There are so many network marketing trainers and trainings, but none are as powerful as Jesus and the Bible. Everything you need to know about building a business is contained in the pages of this book. If you want me to keep going, I want to talk with you about leadership and how Jesus was different from all the other leaders before him."

"Yes", they said, at the same time.

Jesus as a Leader

Paul excused himself to go to the restroom. As he slid past Tim, Susan began thinking about some of the leaders she had served under. They were mostly demanding tyrants whose motto was *my way or the highway*. She had found them closed to suggestions, input, or ideas. At times they weren't even open to important facts that impacted the situation. In her mind the word leader was synonymous with dictator and she wondered if Jesus was that type of leader. Just then, Paul slipped back into his seat.

"Are you ready to hear about Jesus as a leader?" he asked.

"I am," Tim responded.

"Yes, I am as well," Susan said. "I'm very

interested in hearing about the leadership style that Jesus used, as most of the leaders I've encountered have been dictatorial."

"That's the case with many leaders, but I believe you'll find Jesus' leadership style to be very unique and one that you can model. First, it's important for a leader to have a clear purpose."

Paul opened his Bible and turned to Luke 4:18-19 and read "The Spirit of the Lord is on me, because he has anointed me to preach good news to the poor. He has sent me to proclaim freedom for the prisoners and recovery of sight for the blind, to release the oppressed, to proclaim the year of the Lord's favor." Closing the Bible, he continued by explaining that every good leader has a life purpose. It's their 'why' for going through life. Purpose becomes the driving force that enables a good leader to work through the tough times.

"I've always wondered why everyone talks about purpose so much in network marketing," Tim interjected.

"It's critical to long term success. Have you determined your life purpose?"

"No, I've always just sort of taken life as it came to me."

"If you take life as it comes to you, then you will always operate in a reactionary mode and eventually you'll wear down and give up."

"Yeah, that's pretty much where I am now."

"Then there's no better time than the present to discover your purpose," he said, smiling at the young man. "Tell me, what really gets you excited. I mean really passionate?"

"Well, I dunno . . . I guess helping people."

"How?"

"Well, I've had a couple times when I went downtown with a group from our church and fed the homeless. That really felt good."

"So, would you say you are passionate about helping the homeless?"

Tim smiled. "Well, not just the homeless, but the poor too."

"I believe you're unveiling your purpose and it's right in line with what Jesus told us to do here on earth."

"So, my purpose is to help the homeless and the poor?"

"I believe it's a bit more detailed than that. What's been on your heart for years?"

"Uh, well I've always wanted to have a building where I could house the homeless and help them become productive members of society and on fire disciples of Jesus Christ."

"There you go, that's your purpose. So, what are you going to need to accomplish that purpose?"

"Uh, a big building, lots of money, and the time to do it."

"Can your network marketing business provide all that?"

"Yeah. I guess I never thought about it that way. So, if I build my business, it will provide the income and the free time."

"You've got it!"

"Susan, how about you?"

"Mine isn't quite as grandiose as Tim's. My parents will turn seventy this year and they've had a pretty difficult life. I'd like to buy them a new home and set up an account that will take care of them for the remainder of their lives."

"That's great, but I think there's more to it. Something bigger perhaps?"

"Well, when I was a teenager, I helped out at a nursing home and was saddened by all the people who were all alone. I've always wanted to set up a non-profit organization that matches younger people with those in the nursing homes who have no family in the area. They would visit weekly and take them out to do things ever so often. They would also bring flowers and gifts for special occasions. Most of all they would bring love back into lonely lives."

"Now we're talking."

"Can you see how network marketing could help you accomplish your purpose?"

She nodded. "Yes, I can and I'm excited to get going."

"So, the first thing we can learn from Jesus about leadership is that leaders have a personal purpose that drives them. Sometimes this purpose is also referred to as vision and the Bible says that where there is no vision, people perish. I believe that's one of the reasons that so many people fail in network marketing – they don't have a reason to keep going through the tough times. I'm excited that both of you now have a purpose."

Paul continued by sharing that most people get into network marketing for the money and that when you chase money it will always run faster, but if you run toward your purpose, the blessings of money will chase you down. Successful leaders are always part of something that is bigger than themselves and their own needs and wants. That's one of the reasons why people want to follow them.

Once again, he opened his Bible and turned to Mark 3:13-19 and read, "Jesus went up on a mountainside and called to him those he wanted, and they came to him. He appointed twelve—designating them apostles—that they might be with him and that he might send them out to preach and to have authority to drive out demons. These are the twelve he appointed: Simon (to whom he gave the name Peter) James son of Zebedee and his brother John (to them he gave the name Boanerges, which means Sons of Thunder), Andrew, Philip, Bartholomew, Matthew, Thomas, James son of Alphaeus, Thaddaeus, Simon the Zealot and Judas Iscariot, who betrayed him."

"I mentioned earlier, one of the biggest myths in network marketing is that you should sponsor anyone who can fog a mirror. In this example of leadership, we see that Jesus selected twelve from those who were following him. As you build your network, be selective about who you sponsor. Pick people who you like and would enjoy working with. Select those who get excited by the concept and who also have a big purpose or vision. As we can see in Jesus, a leader doesn't always look for the most talented, but rather those who are willing to follow."

"Man, I think I've done everything a person could do wrong in this business," Tim said, shaking his head.

"The good news is that you can now start doing everything right and you'll be amazed at how quickly things will turn around. Okay, let's continue on to our next lesson from Jesus as leader."

Paul turned in his Bible to John 15:15 and read, "I no longer call you servants, because a servant does not know his master's business. Instead, I have called you friends, for everything that I learned from my Father I have made known to you." He continued by explaining that every good leader creates a friend culture in his or her network. As Jesus did, he treated them as friends, rather than as downline members, because friends are more loyal and work harder to achieve common goals.

"So, as you build your networks, become friends with those you sponsor. Get to know them personally. Find out about their lives and what makes them tick. Discover their life purpose and do everything you can to help them accomplish it. On the same token, share your life and purpose with them. If you build a network of friends, you will quickly accomplish your purpose and enjoy the journey."

"That makes so much sense," Susan interjected. "In the corporate world, leaders never befriend their employees and so there is very little loyalty."

"That's one of the great advantages of network marketing over the corporate world. Because those in your downline are not your employees, you can develop close and intimate friendships, as Jesus did with his disciples."

"Seems like it would be a lot more fun to go on

this journey with a bunch of friends."

"You're absolutely correct. Some of my best friends are people in my downline. When you create this culture, if they don't start out as friends, they quickly become one. In fact, my wife and I do a great deal of traveling with our downline, both for business and pleasure. We absolutely love to walk the beaches of the world with our friends and network marketing has provided both the funds and the free time to do exactly that."

"Wow! That's what I want to do," Tim exclaimed.

"Well then, develop a network of friends and help them become successful. Now, let's look at a couple more lessons on leadership that we can learn from Jesus. First, he loved his followers unconditionally. We see that particularly with Peter. Even though Peter did some crazy things and even denied knowing the Lord three times, Jesus continued to love him. He even loved Judas, who betrayed him. That's a common trait among top leaders – they love people unconditionally."

"Next, leaders are transparent. Jesus allowed his disciples to see him tired, hungry, and angry. A good leader will talk about his or her struggles and weaknesses, so that people can more easily relate."

"That's a very good point," Susan added. "I have appreciated leaders who showed weakness, but still succeed. It made me feel better about myself."

"You're absolutely right. If a leader looks perfect and infallible, then people will think of him or her as unapproachable and their position unattainable."

"Okay, the final aspect of leadership that Jesus

modeled is that leaders are action-oriented. They don't just sit around and expect other people to do the work. Even though he was tired, and it was difficult at times, Jesus went out among the people and his disciples followed. He fed, healed, delivered, and raised people from the dead. Jesus taught, rebuked, and modeled. He was all about action and so is every great leader."

"I don't understand that one, because for several years I've been working my tail off and yet I have very little to show for all that work," Tim bemoaned.

"The key is productive action. Jesus had a purpose and he never wasted any action. Everything moved him toward the fulfillment of his purpose. Now that you have a purpose, your actions will produce much better results."

"I hope so," he responded.

"Okay, so who can tell me what we've learned by looking at Jesus as a leader?"

"Leaders always have a purpose or vision which is bigger than their personal wants and needs," Susan answered. "Plus, they're selective with who they recruit."

"Very good; what else?"

"A good leader develops a network of friends and loves them unconditionally," Tim added.

"Excellent!"

"Good leaders are transparent by sharing their personal struggles and weaknesses, so people can relate," Susan offered.

"That's great! Anything else?"

"Action," Tim said.

"Perfect. If you follow Jesus' example of leadership and do these things, you will build a very successful network marketing business and enjoy life with many good and loyal friends. Now . . . anyone want to know the greatest secret to success?"

The Greatest Secret

After a short stretch and restroom break, Paul continued, "Okay, let's talk about the greatest secret."

"Are you talking about that DVD and book I saw on TV a few years ago?" Susan asked.

"No, I'm talking about the real secret. Many books, videos, and teachers have taught parts of the real secret, leaving the one true God out of it. They are convinced that if they practice such teachings, they will be more like God. That's the same deception that Satan used in the Garden of Eden with Eve. It worked then and it's still working today, as millions have and millions more will continue to be deceived by such erroneous teachings."

"But what about all the people who have followed all these secret teachings and have seen miraculous changes in their lives?"

"Don't misunderstand me, there is some veiled truth within these teachings and at times it will produce short-lived successes, but because, as John 10:10 says, 'the thief comes only to steal, kill, and destroy', Satan might allow people to prosper for awhile, but if the teaching is not completely based on the Bible, everything is built on sand and eventually it will lead to destruction. This is why we see so many people gain wealth and then either squander it or commit suicide."

"I know a number of Christians, even a Pastor, who think that these teachings are from God and are promoting it to other Christians," Tim said.

"I've encountered this myself. It's sad and unfortunate, but expected," Paul stated.

Susan cocked her head. "How so?"

Paul smiled, flipped through his Bible to a page, and responded. "2 Peter 2:1-3 reads, 'But there were also false prophets among the people, just as there will be false teachers among you. They will secretly introduce destructive heresies, even denying the sovereign Lord who bought them—bringing swift destruction on themselves. Many will follow their depraved conduct and will bring the way of truth into disrepute. In their greed these teachers will exploit you with fabricated stories. Their condemnation has long been hanging over them, and their destruction has not been sleeping.'"

He went on to explain, "Satan is aware of the shortness of time and has ramped up his effort to deceive people, even Christians. The Bible says that Satan comes as an angel of light, appearing to be a messenger of God, but with evil intent. Many people think that they have heard from God, even had conversations with God, when in reality they were speaking with the devil."

"Now hold on here, are we talking about that guy in the red suit with a pitchfork?"

Paul chuckled and then answered, "No, that's just a cartoon version that someone made up. The devil or satan is a fallen angel. He and one third of the angels rebelled against God, were defeated and cast out of heaven. They now have a mission to steal from, kill, and destroy mankind."

"So, you said that people speak with the devil?"

"Well, not like you and I are speaking. The devil is a spiritual being, so you can't see him, and he doesn't use an audible voice. Rather, he whispers thoughts that you might think are from God or even from your own mind."

"Ok, then how do we differentiate between the devil's whispers, God's voice, and our own mind?"

"The answer is the Bible. If the thought lines up with the Bible, then it's God or one of his messenger angels. However, if it doesn't, then it is a demonic presence speaking – one that is intent on destruction or perhaps your mind. This is why it's so important to read, study, meditate in, and memorize the Word of God. If it is firmly planted in a person's heart, they will more easily recognize the counterfeit when it comes along."

"Okay, I'm confused, is that the real secret?" Tim asked.

"I'm getting there. Psalm 23:7 in the King James Version of the Bible says, 'For as he thinketh in his heart, so is he' and that is the real secret to success."

"Huh, I don't get it."

"Basically, God has made you in such a way that you move toward what you think about most. So, if you think about failing, you will fail. However, if you think about success, you will succeed."

"That's all it takes, is thinking?"

"No, that's just the start."

"Let's talk about how the mind works. First, when we think about something, a picture is created. For example, if you were to think about a pink elephant, that is the picture created in your mind. You wouldn't see the words *pink* and *elephant*, rather you would see a picture or movie of a pink elephant."

"Whoa, that's crazy, I just saw a pink elephant plodding along with his trunk swaying back and forth."

"It works every time. Thoughts about your network marketing business will also create pictures. Negative thoughts will create negative images and positive thoughts will result in positive images. The key is to use your thoughts to plant the proper images, because those images will result in paradigms. A paradigm is a pattern of thinking."

Tim looked at the floor and sighed, "I've really failed in this area. Most of my thoughts are negative. I guess that's why I'm such a failure."

"You just did it again. Remember the greatest secret is that you become what you think about and speak out of your mouth. You just said you were a failure. Change your thinking and what comes out of your mouth and you will start enjoying success."

"It's so hard, but I'll do my best to change. I really want to be successful."

"That's great. This is the reason so many people never seem to succeed at anything – they have created a paradigm of failure. The best way to describe this process is that the pictures are like still frames in a movie. When they all come together it produces the moving picture, which is called a paradigm."

"I've read about paradigms," Susan responded.

"Past teaching and experiences all contribute to your paradigms, so check them to see if they are in line with God's promises in the Bible. For example, many people have developed a paradigm of poverty. They've been taught either directly or indirectly that people with money are not godly. Perhaps they've even developed the paradigm that money is the root of evil, but the Bible says that the love of money is the root of evil. Money is nothing more than a tool that can be used for good or bad. However, if you love money more than God, then you have the wrong paradigm."

"Paradigms produce programs. The brain is much like a computer, as it requires programs to operate properly. Now fortunately, people don't have to load a bunch of software in some port in the back of their heads, as the programs are all hardware based. Everything necessary was loaded in the brain at birth. As the brain collects data from paradigms, it sets these programs to run unconsciously. Now, to make sure that the programs are lined up with the Word of God, it's important to do what is instructed in Romans 12:2, "be transformed by the renewing of your mind." Read the Bible every day, it will create better pictures, paradigms, and programs.

"Okay, so what does all this have to do with network marketing?" Tim asked.

"Many Christians struggle in network marketing because they have incorrect programs running about money and wealth. Jeremiah 29:11 promises that God has a plan for each person – a plan to prosper them. Deuteronomy 8:18 says that God has given each of us the ability to gain wealth. Proverbs 13:21 promises that prosperity is the reward of the righteous. Clearly God wants His children prosperous and if a person has the right programs running, God will use network marketing to produce wealth. Why? So that as the Apostle Paul says in 2 Corinthians 9:10, we can be 'generous on every given occasion.'"

"So, God actually wants us to be wealthy?" Susan asked.

"That's what the Word of God says. However, not at the expense of His love, so God will only allow as much wealth as you can handle. He never wants money to destroy His kids."

"Although I've never heard it taught, I always thought the church believed it was sort of holy to be poor," Tim added.

"That is the paradigm in many churches, which is why so many of them are doing poorly. However, the truth is that God has a plan to prosper His children, so that they can channel the money back into Kingdom building on earth."

Tim grinned and said, "That really is a paradigm shift for me."

"That paradigm shift will now change the programs that have kept you from prospering in network marketing. Plus, the programs will change your expectations. Why don't you tell us about your current expectations in network marketing?"

"Well, when I first joined, I had high expectations, but as time has gone by, my expectations have changed."

"How so?"

"Because most of the time things haven't work the way I wanted, so I began to expect failure."

"That's quite common and another of the reasons why so many people fail in network marketing."

He continued by explaining, "all expectations are produced by the programs running in your brain and expectations are directly responsible for success or failure. Matthew 9:29 says, 'According to your faith will it be done to you.' As you meditate over the Word of God, the pictures in your mind begin to change, which changes the paradigms, programs, and expectations. Through that process your faith is built, and that faith will open doors for God to work in your life."

"The key is that because of the free will God gave man, He can only respond to the level of your expectations. For example, if you expect God to come in at the last minute and provide just enough to pay that looming mortgage payment, then He will do just that. However, if you serve an abundant God and expect abundance, based on God's promises, then you will receive abundance in every area of your life."

"I've found that to be so true," Susan interjected. "In my career, I've only risen as high as I expected."

"You're right. We can only go as high as our expectations, not because God doesn't want us any higher, but because we've limited His ability to help us."

"That's amazing!" Tim said. "I thought God could do anything?"

"He can, but He chooses not to override our free will, even when He knows it would be better for us. God wants us to learn lessons that will build our character, so we can properly handle everything He gives us. Okay, would you like to continue with the process?"

"YES," they exclaimed at the same time.

"I like your enthusiasm. Your expectations will result in actions. If you are expecting failure, the programs running will instruct your body to do the things that will ensure failure. On the other hand, if you're expecting success, then the programs will lead your body to do things that will result in success. Results are the final step. No matter what actions you take, you will get results. Positive actions produce positive results and negative actions produce negative results."

"So, if I understand this correctly, the key is to start with positive thoughts that eventually lead to positive actions, but what if your thoughts tend to be more on the negative side?" Susan asked.

"Our world tends to be more negative than

positive, so it's important to limit the negative by minimizing that input. I choose not to look at the worldly news, because so much of it is negative. I'm also very careful about what television shows and movies I watch. Along with that I limit my exposure to social media and negative people."

"Beyond just limiting the negative, it's important to fill your mind with the positive, which is the Word of God. I devote time first thing in the morning to reading and meditating over the scriptures. I also read the Bible as the last thing I do before sleeping. That way I'm filling my mind with pictures straight from the promises of God. If a negative thought tries to creep in, I immediately reach up, grab it, and cast it away." Paul said, smiling at Tim, who also reached up to grab the invisible thought.

"So, is that it? That's the greatest secret?" Tim asked, with a disappointed tone. "I was expecting something bigger."

"This is bigger than you can imagine. Lining up your thoughts and expectations with God's will produce amazing results. Keep in mind that He is the Creator of all things and that He thought about our world before He spoke it into existence. Since we are made in God's image, our thoughts are just as powerful. That's why these secret teachings are so destructive, because the real secret is that we are already made in God's likeness and image. We already have the character of God and the ability to think and have those thoughts manifest into actions and positive results. All we need to do is mold our thinking with the Bible, so that proper paradigms are created, which will result in powerful programs dictating our expectations and actions. If we do this, we will enjoy positive results."

"I think I'm getting it," he responded, with a grin.

"Good, because this will dramatically change your business and life. Now, there's one more powerful, life changing key to this whole process. Are you ready for more?

They both smiled and said, "absolutely!"

Nine

The Power of the Tongue

Paul responded to their enthusiastic desire to hear more, "great, then let's open the Bible to Genesis 1:3."

He proceeded to read, "Then God said, 'Let there be light' and there was light." He then moved down to verse six and read, "Then God said, 'Let there be space between the waters, to separate the waters of the heavens from the waters of the earth.' And that is what happened." Paul finished by reading verse fourteen, "Then God said, 'Let great lights appear in the sky to separate the day from the night.'"

"What do you see that these three verses have in common?"

"God is creating things," Tim answered.

"That's true, but not quite what I'm looking for.

How about you, Susan, any ideas?"

"No clue."

"In all three cases, God spoke things into existence, and from that we're going to learn about one of the most powerful tools in network marketing."

"Huh? I don't get it. What does God speaking things into existence have to do with network marketing?" Tim asked.

"Good question, but I want to see if either of you can guess."

"Could it have something to do with speaking?" Susan responded.

"Bingo! That's the million-dollar answer. Let's go back to the Bible for the next clue."

Paul turned to James 3:4-5 and shared about the tongue. "The scripture reads: 'And a small rudder makes a huge ship turn wherever the pilot chooses to go, even though the winds are strong. In the same way, the tongue is a small thing that makes grand speeches.' The tongue is one of the keys to network marketing success. More often than not, it's the sole determiner for success or failure, as it controls the direction of a person's life, much as a rudder controls the direction of a ship. Verse six continues the teaching, 'But a tiny spark can set a great forest on fire. And the tongue is a flame of fire. It is a whole world of wickedness, corrupting your entire body. It can set your whole life on fire, for it is set on fire by hell itself.'"

"These are harsh words, but very true. I spent many years failing in my marriage, relationships, and business because I couldn't control my tongue."

"I know, I've had my share of doozies," Tim said. "My tongue has put me in the doghouse more times than I can count."

"I must agree," Susan said. "My husband and I have had some big fights and said things we later regretted."

"The answer to handling the monster in your mouth is found earlier in the book of James in chapter one and verse five, which says, 'If you need wisdom, ask our generous God and he will give it to you.' In order to tame the tongue, you will need the guidance of the Holy Spirit who lives in you."

"By sharing how he learned to tame his tongue by asking God for wisdom. Early in his marriage there were many times when his wife would say something that pushed a button and so he responded by saying something that would push one of her buttons. This would escalate until they were screaming at each other and when the fight was over, they wouldn't talk for a day or two. This became a vicious pattern in their marriage, which resulted in Paul demanding that they go to counseling. However, the counseling didn't change things and they considered the possibility of divorce. Fortunately, they decided to stick it out and later, after accepting Christ and attending a Christian marriage conference, they learned how to control the tongue through God's wisdom.

"Wow, I'd love to know how to do that in my marriage," Tim responded.

"I would as well," Susan added.

"It took time, but I learned to ask the Holy Spirit for guidance before I responded. A common saying out in the world is 'engage brain before engaging tongue,' but in the spirit realm it would go more like this, 'engage the Holy Spirit before engaging tongue.' When my wife or anyone else in my life would say something that pushed one of my buttons, rather than immediately respond, I would quietly ask the Holy Spirit to guide me and either I would say nothing or would say what the Lord offered to my mind. It was an amazing transition and had a dramatic impact on all my relationships."

"I've never really felt like I hear from God," Tim responded.

"Have you ever lost your keys or something else and after looking for awhile, suddenly knew exactly where they were?"

"Yeah, I guess so," Tim answered.

"That was the Holy Spirit speaking to you."

"The Holy Spirit, huh? I thought my memory just finally kicked in."

"The Holy Spirit is speaking to us all the time – giving us direction in every part of life. The key is to get tuned into the right frequency. Now, you're probably wondering what all this has to do with network marketing; am I right?"

Tim grinned. "Yeah, I was just thinking that."

"Yes, I'm interested in knowing how the tongue can determine my success or failure in business," Susan added.

"We're going to examine two areas that will impact your business. The first, I mentioned earlier and that is speaking the Word of God into your circumstances. The Bible is filled with God's instructions and promises for your life. That's why it's so important to meditate over the scriptures every day, so that they become firmly planted in your heart and when trouble comes, you will naturally begin to speak those scriptures that apply."

"Can you give us some examples?" Susan asked.

"Let's say you're having financial struggles. The bills are due and there isn't enough money. Those are the circumstances. However, the Bible says, in Philippians 4:19, 'And my God will meet all your needs according to his glorious riches in Christ Jesus.' This is a promise that, when you are obedient to God, he will take care of your needs. You can stand on that promise and begin to speak that to your financial situation. You could also speak Jeremiah 29:11, 'For I know the plans I have for you,' declares the LORD, 'plans to prosper you and not to harm you, plans to give you hope and a future.' Is this making sense?"

"Perfect sense."

"Yeah," Tim added.

"Now let's see how this will relate to your network marketing business. Deuteronomy 8:18 says, 'But remember the LORD your God, for it is He who gives you the ability to produce wealth, and so confirms His covenant, which He swore to your forefathers, as it is today.' So, if He has given you the ability to produce wealth and you are not wealthy, that means either God is a liar, which we know He isn't, or you aren't using your ability properly. Once again, we need to call on the Holy Spirit for wisdom on how to use our ability to produce wealth. As I talked about earlier, the Spirit will give you that Eden Factor idea for your business that will result in wealth."

"I'm not quite tracking with you," Tim said.

"If you ask, the Holy Spirit might give you the name of a person who will become a top leader in your network or He might instruct you to go to a certain place, where you will meet a key person. You might receive insight on a new place to advertise and find that it brings you many excellent new associates. Can you see how that could happen?"

"Yes, now that makes sense," he responded.

"Okay, so the first powerful way you can use your tongue is to speak the Word of God into your business and all aspects of your life. The second application can be found in Proverbs 18:21, 'The tongue has the power of life and death, and those who love it will eat its fruit.' Early in my network marketing career I was constantly speaking death to my business. I would complain about the company, products, and particularly my sponsor and upline leaders. My failure was always someone else's fault. Then I learned about the power of the tongue and began speaking life into my business."

"How did you do that?" Susan asked.

"Instead of complaining, I would speak about my business as I wanted it to be. In Romans 4:17 it says that God calls things that are not as though they were. In other words, God speaks what is to become. Since we are made in the image and likeness of God, we have that same creative power in our tongue. In the Bible, Abram called things that were not as though they were. After God promised him a large extended family and changed his name to Abraham, which meant father of nations, Abraham began to speak of himself in that way."

"I followed that example and began to say things like 'I have a large international network that produces a high six-figure income, which gives me total financial and time freedom' and 'I have many great self-sufficient leaders who are among my closest friends.' Can you see the difference that would make versus complaining all the time?"

"I can see the difference, but I don't understand how it works."

"When you speak in line with the Word of God, your words go into the spirit realm and God responds by sending angels to produce what you are speaking. The Holy Spirit will prompt you into action, in accordance with what the angels have arranged and the results will seem miraculous. Does that make sense?"

"I never realized that my words had so much power," Tim said.

"Words are incredibly powerful, but most people don't realize it and so they allow words to destroy their marriages, relationships, finances, and network marketing businesses. If you speak the Word of God over your business and you speak about your business as you want it to be, you will be amazed at what happens to your business and income. Now, I want to tell you why, contrary to much of the network marketing training, you should rarely follow the crowd."

The Crowd is Almost Always Wrong

P aul gave them a sly smile and said, "we're in the home stretch. Just a couple more key pieces. The first is going to be a bit of a shocker. The crowd is almost always wrong.

"Now, that doesn't make any sense to me," said Tim. "I've always been taught to do whatever my upline does, isn't that following the crowd?"

"I know that is the prevailing thought in network marketing and there is nothing wrong with listening to your upline and using their systems, particularly if they are Christians. If they aren't, then you must compare what they are teaching to the Bible. Proverbs 19:12 teaches, 'Many are the plans in a man's heart, but it is the LORD's purpose that prevails.' If we aren't operating in God's plan, then whatever we do will fail."

"So, how do we know when it's God's plan?" Susan asked.

"We can gain some insight into His general plan for our lives by reading the Bible. It tells us to be salt and light in the world. That means we are to be different, in a good way, from the rest of the folks. He wants us to take care of the poor, orphans, and widows. We are to go and make disciples, which means to tell people about Jesus and when they accept him, help them down the new path. We know that God has a plan to prosper us, which means that if we are operating our network marketing businesses using God's plan, we will be successful. That brings us to our individual plan and that you will have to seek in prayer."

"Being a new Christian, I'm not really sure how to pray."

"You're just having a conversation with God, only you won't hear his voice like you hear mine. Rather it will seem to come up from inside you – like a voice in your head. Then you just have to make sure that it's God and not Satan."

"How will I know the difference?" she asked.

"As I mentioned earlier, Satan's mission on earth is to steal, kill, and destroy, so if the voice is telling you to doubt or question or is overly negative, then it's the devil at work. God's voice will be encouraging and give you wisdom and direction that always lines up with the Bible."

"So, do I just ask God about my business?"

"Yes, it's that simple. God clearly brought this

network marketing business into your life, so all you have to do is ask him for the plan. Then as you are introduced to new things, ask if they are part of God's plan. If you don't have peace in your heart about something you're considering, then don't do it."

"I'm not fully understanding what this has to do with following the crowd," Tim interjected.

"For the most part, the crowd is doing things the world's way and who did Jesus call the prince of this world?"

"Satan?"

"That's right. So if the crowd is using a system that was designed by Satan, what is his ultimate intent?"

"To steal, kill, and destroy."

"Correct! So, does it make sense to follow the crowd, unless they are following Jesus?"

"I guess not."

"You see, following the crowd is like rowing a boat downstream. It's easy and it seems like everything is going really well. The only problem is that unbeknownst to you, there is a huge waterfall up ahead. If you don't stop and row back upstream, you're going to die. Most of the world is rowing downstream, heading for disaster and they don't even know it. Our job is two-fold: First to row upstream and second to tell everyone else to follow us, as we follow Jesus. That goes for every part of our lives."

"That seems like it makes life much more difficult," Susan commented.

"Yes, it does make it more difficult in one way,

but easier in another."

"How so?"

"Well, you're going to take some flak from those people who are operating in the world's system. They're depending on their business or job as their source of income and possibly are doing well at the moment. However, the majority of them are heading toward a financial disaster and don't know it. It could be losing their job or a large account or a big drop in the stock market. Whatever it is, they won't be expecting it and it will take them down – that's Satan's plan for all the people operating in the world's system."

"If that's the case, then we need to warn them," Tim said.

"Yes, we do, but that's part of the difficulty of rowing upstream, because most of them are going to think you're crazy and won't listen. However, keep in mind that your job is just to inform them and plant the seed that there is a better system – God's system and it will never fail."

"I'm still a bit confused. Can you give us some examples of God's system in network marketing?" Susan asked.

"God's system for building a network marketing business is through love – get your eyes off the money and materialism that is so pervasive in the network marketing industry and instead, focus on making friends and helping others succeed. The more you give the more God will give to you. Have a servant's heart and help even those not in your downline. Serving others will open the door for God to work miraculously in your business. So, instead of thinking of people as prospects, think of them as friends you can help."

"What does that look like?"

"Instead of approaching people with your business and excitedly blurting out all the facts and figures, ask questions about their lives. I can explain one of my favorite approaches by using the acrostic FORM. The *F* stands for Family and so you ask questions about their family. The *O* is Occupation, and you ask questions about their job or business. The *R* stands for Recreation, so you ask questions about what they like to do for fun and their next vacation. The *M* is Money, and you ask them about investments, retirement, and ways to make extra money. The whole idea is to uncover pain areas."

"Pain areas, what do you mean?" Tim asked.

"For example, let's say you're asking questions about a man's family and you discover that he's working long hours at the job, which keeps him from seeing his son's baseball games. That's a pain area."

"I see, so what would be an example in the occupation area?" he asked.

"Can either of you think of a good example?"

"If I was speaking with a woman executive who had hit the glass ceiling, would that be a pain area?" Susan asked.

"Very good. Any others?"

"What if there was the possibility of the person losing their job?" Tim asked.

"Excellent! Sounds like you're both getting this. The reason for uncovering the pain areas is so that you can present your business as a solution. So, let's look at a full example. You're speaking with Jerry and he owns a plumbing business. Jerry works long, hard hours every week and he's starting to feel the pains of crawling under people's sinks and kneeling on the floor. He has two children he doesn't see as much as he'd like. Plus, he can't really afford to take a vacation, because if he isn't working, there isn't any income. Money is always tight and because there have been a few lean years, Jerry has quite a bit of debt, which is creating stress between he and his wife. By introducing your business to Jerry as a solution to these pain areas, he and his wife are more likely to be interested, because you have shown an interest in their life."

"It's that old saying, 'people don't care how much you know, until they know how much you care,'" Susan added.

"That's it in a nutshell. If you show that you care about people's lives, by asking questions and then presenting your business as a solution, your recruiting percentages will skyrocket. Then, as you actually help them alleviate the problems through the network marketing business, you will develop loyal friends."

"So, if I'm understanding this entire concept, it's best not to do what everyone else is doing. Instead of approaching people directly with the business, we should ask questions and uncover the pain areas, so that when we present network marketing it will be a solution to their issues. Am I on track?"

"You've got it. If every network marketer takes this type of approach, they will enjoy greater success and the industry will have a much better reputation."

"I can certainly see that, as I've been prospected for network marketing by friends and family members in the past and was totally turned off. However, if someone had approached me in the way you've described, I probably would have joined years ago."

The conversation was suddenly interrupted by a voice over the intercom, "We are starting our final descent and will be landing in Maui in approximately twenty-five minutes. The flight attendants will be coming through the cabin to pick up any trash."

"Wow, the time has really gone by fast," Tim blurted.

"Time does pass quickly when you're having fun," Susan added, "I can't believe we're almost there."

"We have one more topic. Would you like to wrap this up before we land?"

"Yes," Tim responded.

"Absolutely," Susan added.

Vision, Purpose, and Goals

Paul again opened his Bible and read Proverbs 29:18 to Tim and Susan, "Where there is no vision, the people perish."

As he finished, the flight attendant arrived, and the three travelers handed him their trash. Susan had noticed that he was always smiling and really seemed to enjoy his job. She smiled and handed him an empty plastic cup.

"You have a great attitude," she said to him.

"Thanks, I try. It's hard sometimes."

"Oh, why is that?"

"The passengers aren't always the nicest people."

"I fly often and can certainly attest to that. Even considering some unpleasant people, you seem to really enjoy your job."

"It pays the bills," he responded collecting the trash from Paul and Tim.

"Not exactly your dream job?"

"No, I'd really like to go back to school and be an architect, but I don't have the money."

"That's a great profession."

"Yeah and they earn a lot of money too."

"I'm Susan," she said, reaching her hand across her fellow travelers.

"Julio," he replied, firmly shaking her hand.

"Nice handshake. Very professional. Tell me Julio, if I could show you a way to earn the extra money you need for school, without jeopardizing your job with the airlines, would you be interested?"

"Yeah, I guess."

"Before I leave the plane, would you please give me your full name, email address, and phone number, so I can send you some information and follow up to answer questions?"

"Sure, but what's it all about?"

"The company I'm working with is exploding and looking for talented, ambitious people like yourself. It would take more time than we have to explain, so I'll send you the information, which will give you all the details. Then we can talk on the phone and I'll answer any remaining questions. How does that sound?"

"Sounds good. I've got to collect the rest of the trash, but I'll get you my information before we land."

"Thanks, Julio. I look forward to the possibility

of working with you to help you achieve your dream of becoming an architect."

"Thanks," he said, turning to the people in the next row.

"Wow, you're good," Tim said. "Glad you're on my team," he added with a grin.

"Thanks, that was easier than I expected and it felt really natural."

"Susan, that was marvelous and a great lead into my final topic. As you spoke with Julio, you uncovered his dream. Everyone has a dream. Sometimes it's been buried under the muck of the world, but it's there if you just dig a bit. Dreams are just part of a bigger vision and purpose. However, before we go into that, I want to discuss the scripture I just read."

He then shared how so many people are walking through life like zombies from a horror movie. They mindlessly react to whatever comes across their path and yet the reality is that God has a huge vision that includes them. God's vision is to bring every living person into His Kingdom through belief in Jesus Christ as their Savior. His vision also includes prospering His children, so that they can enjoy life to the fullest.

"If that's the case, how come so many people are struggling?" Tim asked.

"Remember that Satan is alive and well on planet earth and he has a bad plan for every single person. He's mad at God for kicking him out of heaven and he's taking it out on mankind."

"Why was Satan kicked out of heaven?" Susan inquired.

"Pride caused him to think that he was greater than God and so he led a rebellion, which was quickly repelled by the archangel Michael and the remaining angels. God then expelled him from heaven."

"And why is he taking it out on us?" she asked.

"Because we are God's prize creation and His children. Satan is jealous of us."

"I believe I'm starting to see this picture more clearly. It goes back to Eden, when God created the perfect world for mankind. His vision is to re-create that world for us, but Satan stands in the way, am I on the right track?"

"Actually, Satan has already been defeated by Jesus dying on the cross, but he's still present and doing his best to limit God's vision on earth. Satan doesn't have any real power, except when people allow him to manipulate their thoughts and actions into sin, which opens the door for him to steal, kill, and destroy."

"But, I thought you said that all sin was forgiven?"

"It is, but unfortunately many people, even Christians, don't truly believe and so they inadvertently allow Satan to control their lives through guilt and condemnation."

"Yeah, I've had my share of that," Tim interjected.

"Haven't we all. The great part is that we don't have to accept the guilt and condemnation, because as the Bible says in Romans 8:1, 'There is now no condemnation for those who are in Christ Jesus.' It's up to us, but if we receive the guilt and condemnation, we will be paralyzed and unable to fulfill our part in achieving God's vision for the world."

"Why does God need us? Isn't he all powerful?" Susan asked.

"Yes, He is all powerful, but because He gave dominion of the earth to mankind, God utilizes us to achieve His vision."

"Wow, I never realized that," Tim said. "I just figured if God couldn't find someone to do it, He'd do it himself."

"God could, but He won't. That's why it's so important for each of us to do our part and why the Bible says that we will perish without vision. We are nothing without God's vision. Does that make sense?"

"Yes," they replied in unison.

Once again, a voice over the intercom interrupted their conversation, "We are about fifteen minutes away from Maui. Those of you sitting on the right side of the plane should have a nice view of the islands in just a few minutes. At this time, we will need you to turn off all electronic devices and place your seatbacks in the upright position with tray tables up and locked in place. The flight crew will be through the cabin one last time to pick up any remaining trash."

Paul continued, "now, once we understand God's vision, the next step is to uncover our purpose. This is your individual reason for being on this earth. If you haven't already figured it out, you're not here by accident."

"This is all very interesting. I've achieved a high

level of success in my life and yet I've always sensed there was more. That I was meant to accomplish something greater," Susan interjected.

"How did it make you feel not knowing what it was you were to accomplish?"

"At times, I've been frustrated and even angry, but mostly I just wondered why I worked so hard."

"Now we're getting somewhere. Earlier in the flight you both discovered at least a part of your purpose. Tim, you wanted to provide a facility for the homeless and Susan, you want to set up a non-profit organization that matches young people with senior citizens who have no family. Remember how your purpose fits into God's bigger vision?"

"Absolutely," Susan replied.

"Me too," Tim said.

"Once you have the big vision and your purpose clearly in mind, then the next step is to seek God for goals that will help you achieve your purpose. If you were taking a trip from Seattle, Washington to Orlando, Florida by car, you would go through a lot of cities on the way, wouldn't you?"

"Yes," they both replied.

"Would any of those cities between Seattle and Orlando be your ultimate destination?"

"No," Susan answered.

"However, as you reached each city, would you be closer to your final destination?"

"If I was going in the right direction. I always get lost," Tim said sheepishly.

"That's a good point and it will help with this illustration. If we've mapped out our entire journey and we're following the map, then each city would represent a goal on the way to your purpose. Goals are not your purpose, rather just stops along the way. Now, as you so brilliantly pointed out, if we aren't following the map and start going in the wrong direction, we will still experience some cities, but they will not lead us to our ultimate destination of Orlando."

"So, God has a big vision for the entire planet, and He has also given us a purpose, which is part of His vision. If we ask, God will give us the goals along the way to achieving the purpose, is that correct?" Susan asked.

"Perfect. Okay, now let's translate this into network marketing. Tim, your purpose is to help the homeless become highly functioning members of God's kingdom, right?"

"Yeah."

"So, that's your final destination and your starting point is where you are right now in life. Goals will be the steps that get you from here to there and God has given you a network marketing business to provide the funding and time freedom to accomplish your purpose. Can you think of some goals that will help you build your business to that point?"

"Well, uh, I would need to sponsor a lot of people."

"How many?"

"Uh, I don't know."

"Will your sponsor and upline leaders be at the convention?"

"Yeah."

"Then, I would highly recommend that you

figure out a rough estimate of how much money is necessary to fund your center and provide you with total time freedom. Next, find out what level in the company earns that income and ask your upline for the average number of people personally sponsored in order to reach that level. Once you know the number, find out how many people you'll need to prospect in order to have enough presentations to sponsor that many new associates. You'll then need a plan to make those contacts and presentations. Plus, you'll want to work with your upline to train and support those who join your downline. Each of these steps is a goal."

"I've always heard about goal setting, but never knew how to do it."

"Once you have those goals, then you'll need to break them down further into objectives. For example, let's say that your goal is five presentations a week, what will it take to do those presentations?"

"Uh, it depends on how I do them. Our company recommends doing the presentations one-on-one."

"Okay, what will you need in order to do those one-on-one presentations?"

"My upline taught me to do the presentation using one of our brochures, so that it was duplicatable."

"That's good. Then you'll need brochures and you'll have to know the presentation, right?"

"Yeah."

"You'll also need a location, right?"

"Right."

"And how will you keep track of these

presentations?"

"I'll use the calendar on my phone."

"So, you'll need to enter the day, time, and location of the presentation, right?"

"Yeah."

"All of these are objectives that will help you accomplish your goal of five presentations a week. Can you see how this works?"

"Yes," they said simultaneously.

"The final step is implementation. It's great to have vision, purpose, goals, and objectives, but if you don't move into action, you'll never accomplish your God-given purpose. Each day, you should set aside some quiet time with God to receive your objectives for the day. Make and prioritize a list of activities and check them off as you accomplish each objective. This will help you move into action and stay there all day. It will also ensure that you are working on the highest priority objectives at all times. If an activity that isn't on your list presents itself, you'll need to ask God about its priority compared to the list. Chances are good that it won't even make the list and is just Satan's feeble attempt to get you to stray from God's plan."

"I've been a goal setter for most of my life and can attest to its power, as I've accomplished a great deal so far. However, I'm excited to see how powerful this is with God as my partner," Susan commented.

"You'll be amazed!"

The plane bounced a bit as it touched down and the three travelers felt the reverse thrust slowing the huge plane. Soon they had taxied into the gate and a voice over the intercom informed them that they had landed safely on Maui.

"Well, it's been a pleasure flying with both of you. Entering the plane, we were strangers and now I consider us friends."

"This has been so great and exactly what I needed," Tim said, reaching a hand toward Paul.

"Strangers shake hands and friends hug," he said, embracing Tim.

"I can't thank you enough. Although I've achieved much and my life is good, I've felt empty lately and couldn't figure out why. Thanks to you that void is gone and I'm excited about my future," Susan said, gently embracing the older man.

Everyone began walking down the aisle single file. As Susan passed Julio, he handed her a piece of paper and said, "I look forward to hearing from you."

"I'll give you a call within the next day or so," Susan replied.

As they walked out into the terminal, Tim breathed deeply and received a fragrant flower lei from a beautiful Polynesian woman. He looked at Paul, tears in his eyes and said, "Thank you! This chance meeting has changed my life."

"There are no chance meetings, only divine appointments," he replied.

Susan and Tim started toward baggage claim as they heard Paul say, "May the grace of our Lord, Jesus Christ be with you always." They looked behind them, but the stately gray-haired man was nowhere to be seen.

"Where did he go?" Susan asked.

"It appears that we've just had a divine experience," Tim replied. "One that will change the rest of our lives."

Made in the USA
Las Vegas, NV
23 April 2021

21924573R00075